THE EXPLORER'S GUIDE TO ALGONQUIN PARK

TEXT AND PHOTOGRAPHS BY
Michael W. P. Runtz

Stoddart

For Harrison:
may we have the wisdom to ensure that
Algonquin and other wild places eternally
remain for you and all others to explore.

First published in 1993 by Stoddart Publishing Co. Limited
34 Lesmill Road
Toronto, Canada
M3B 2T6
(416) 445-3333

Second printing September 1993.

Canadian Cataloguing in Publication Data
Runtz, Michael, W. P.
The explorer's guide to Algonquin Park
Includes index.
ISBN 0-7737-5571-3
1. Algonquin Provincial Park (Ont.) - Description - Guidebooks.
2. Natural history - Ontario - Algonquin Provincial Park - Guidebooks.
3. Outdoor life - Ontario - Algonquin Provincial Park - guidebooks.
I. Title.
FC3065.A4R87 1993   917.13'147   C92-095638-6
F1059.A4R87 1993

Design: Brant Cowie/ArtPlus Limited
Maps and Plates: Robert A. Bracken
Front Cover Photograph: The Barron River Canyon
Printed and bound in Canada

Stoddart Publishing gratefully acknowledges the support of the Canada Council, Ontario Ministry of Tourism, Culture, and Recreation, Ontario Arts Council, and Ontario Publishing Centre in the development of writing and publishing in Canada.

Contents

Acknowledgements

THERE ARE COUNTLESS PEOPLE over the years who have shared their knowledge and passion for Algonquin Park with me. In particular I must thank Ron Tozer and Dan Strickland for not only tutoring me but also for generously putting up with me over the many years I worked at the old Park Museum.

As well, a sincere thanks to Ron Tozer and Nancy Checko for critically reviewing the text and offering many valuable suggestions. Rory MacKay and Jack Mihell were treasure houses for information on Algonquin's history. Other individuals to whom I am indebted include Larry Weller, Larry Cobb, Graham and Lee Forbes, Bill Crins, Henry Checko, Jack Borrowman, Ernie Martelle, Ron Stephenson, Bill and Richard Swift, and Gerhard Schinke.

Special thanks to Bob Bracken, friend and artist extraordinaire, for the excellent artwork and maps that he produced for this book.

And last but never least, my heartfelt gratitude goes to my wife, Heather, and son, Harrison, for understanding and sharing my love for "the Park."

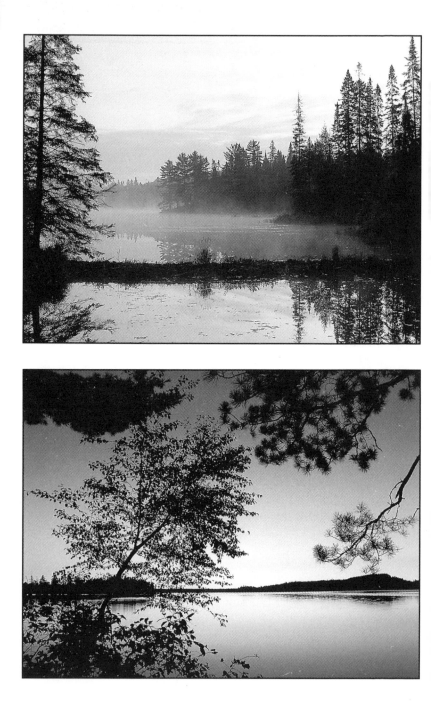

I FELL IN LOVE with Algonquin Park on my very first visit. That was in 1957 when my family came to see the absurdly bold deer which, in those days, drew much attention to the Park. I am sure my parents could never have predicted that from this initial magical excursion an irrepressible obsession would grow.

Many special features set Algonquin Park apart: the maze of sparkling waterways that leads into the wilds; the moose, loons, wolves and other untamed creatures that so readily tolerate our intrusions; the crisp night skies where the aurora dances among the blazing stars. It is also a place where we can share our passion for wilderness with kindred souls.

I have worked many years in Algonquin and have explored its wild recesses as a naturalist, canoeist, biologist and photographer, which has given me a certain familiarity with the Park and its visitors. Over the years the comments and questions of other Park users, ranging from novice campers to serious birders, made it clear there was a real need for a book of this nature. While many of the answers to popular questions could be found in the various excellent Park publications, no single reference pooled the existing information. As well, other specific questions could only be answered by finding the right person to ask or else remained unanswered. This book was written with those needs in mind, and I hope it is an aid to your enjoyment of this incomparable Park.

ACCESSING ALGONQUIN PROVINCIAL PARK

WELCOME TO ALGONQUIN PROVINCIAL PARK, the oldest and second largest park in Ontario. For the past 100 years this magnificent Park has captured the hearts of millions of visitors who have canoed its clear waters and hiked its endless forests. This extraordinary area was formally set aside in 1893, thanks to the efforts and incredible foresight of Alexander Kirkwood and James Dickson. These men, one a government clerk and the other a land surveyor, recognized this highland area as the source of a number of major rivers and the essential habitat for a wide array of wildlife. Water and wildlife, the special features recognized a hundred years ago, are the same attributes that currently attract hundreds of thousands of people annually to the Park.

People are drawn to Algonquin for a number of reasons, one of which is certainly its immense size. With 7,700 square kilometres encompassing endless forests and over a thousand sparkling lakes, the Park offers limitless outdoor recreational opportunities.

Another reason is the amazing diversity of life found here — over 260 species of birds, 40 types of mammals and 1,000 species of plants flourish in the Park. Even more striking is the mixture of species. Southern animals such as white-tailed deer and Scarlet Tanagers occur in proximity to moose and Spruce Grouse, true "northerners." In many ways Algonquin is a naturalist's dream come true.

But why does such a great variety of habitats support a diverse array of flora and fauna? The answer lies in

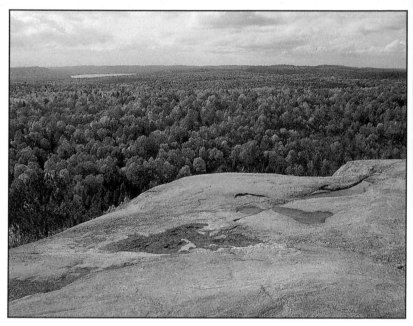

The west side of Algonquin Park is an endless sea of hardwood hills.

the Park's location and in its geological history. Algonquin is situated in a vegetation transition zone where temperatures and the growing season are adequate to support a mixture of plants. Furthermore, the Park is located on a dome where elevations (reaching 585 metres above sea level) intensify temperature extremes, allowing for the establishment of boreal plants.

The last Ice Age also had an important impact on the region. When the glaciers finally retreated a mere 11,000 years ago, a layer of rocks, gravel, sand and silt was deposited over the western highlands. This glacial till traps moisture, which allows hardwood forests to grow. Sugar maple, yellow birch, American beech and ironwood thrive on these hillsides. These hardwood forests change to brilliant hues in the autumn, putting on a show of colour rarely equalled elsewhere.

Great beds of sand, deposited by glacial rivers that flowed through much of the Park's East Side, support a much different forest. This soil fails to trap moisture and thus remains relatively dry. The dry conditions, amplified by a slight rain shadow created by the western uplands, favour the growth of pines and poplars. Trembling aspen and white, red and jack pine forests dominate much of these eastern reaches.

Coniferous forests also abound in other areas. All through Algonquin cool shorelines are fringed by spruces, balsam fir, white cedar and eastern hemlock. Floating sphagnum bogs, wherever solid enough, support the spindly spires of black spruce and the delicate contours of tamarack.

In turn this incredible mosaic of forests sustains the rich array of animal life for which Algonquin is famous. Today the Park is one of the finest moose-viewing areas in the world and boasts one of the most accessible timber wolf populations anywhere. This abundance of life affords excellent photographic opportunities. I speak from personal experience — my first two books, *Algonquin Seasons* and *Moose Country,* are illustrated with photographs taken in Algonquin.

The forests we see nowadays, however, are much different from those encountered by the region's first visitors. Giant white pines towered throughout the western uplands. It was these trees that captured the attention of the early logging industry. As early as the 1830s, axes rang in these forests as the monstrous pines were felled. Thousands of men spent their winters here, cutting the trees, removing the bark and outer wood in a process known as "squaring," and hauling the timbers to frozen lakes. These hardy men lived in the "camboose," a one-room cabin central to the camp. Here they cooked, ate and slept for the duration of the long, cold season. In spring the camps broke up and the timbers were "driven" down swollen rivers to the mighty Ottawa.

By the late 1800s the supply of big pines began to vanish, but a need for other trees soon arose. Smaller trees, undoubtedly scorned by earlier loggers, were eagerly harvested as the demand for sawn lumber quickly grew. New logging camps, more modern in construction than the camboose camps over which they were frequently erected, sprang up over the ensuing years. Logs still thundered down rivers in spring but now also left the newly created Park by rail. And, in addition to logs, the Ottawa, Arnprior and Parry Sound Railway (built between 1894 and 1896 by J. R. Booth, a powerful lumber baron) transported sawn lumber produced in mills located in the Park.

The railway was also important as a means for fishermen and other recreationists to visit Algonquin. As the fame of the Park spread, lodges opened along the line and summer residences appeared on many of the lakes. The highway arrived in the mid-1930s, opening the Park to a different type of user as well as offering an alternate means of transport for the lumber industry. However, when the importance of the railway began to fade and service from the east was stopped in 1946, the great lodges, once thriving enterprises, fell silent and were eventually dismantled. By 1959 all service along this line, previously among the busiest in Canada, was discontinued and a glorious era came to an end. Now only scattered and often obscure clues are all that remain of those early days.

Although Algonquin continues to supply timber to the lumbering industry, it has become far more important as a playground for outdoor recreationists. Today Algonquin provides outstanding camping, canoeing, fishing and wildlife-viewing opportunities. Drive-in campgrounds are not only found along Highway 60, the major access to and the only road crossing the Park, but also at other access points. With over 1,500 Interior campsites along the 1,600 kilometres of established canoe routes and 170 kilometres of backpacking trails, a wilder, more private style of camping is also available. Fish, most notably speckled and lake trout, thrive in the clear, cold waters, and fishermen frequently depart with the proof to support their fantastic stories.

For the explorer who simply appreciates a beautiful area Algonquin will not disappoint. Throughout the Park crystal lakes and winding rivers are fringed with rugged cliffs and fragrant conifers. After cool nights near summer's end, these low-lying areas are smothered with heavy mists. In autumn western slopes flame with vivid colour, and as this show begins to fade the golds of poplars and tamaracks reign supreme. Later, the sparkling snows of winter also create dramatic splendour. In fact, year-round the Park exhibits ever-changing personae that are frequently unrivalled in brilliance or mood.

Algonquin Provincial Park is a very special place. Although a variety of activities have come and gone since the Park's inception, the very fabric of Algonquin has survived intact. Loons still serenade the setting sun and pines continue to whisper secrets to the wind. Today's explorer can enjoy the natural wonders of the present as well as marvel at artifacts from the past.

Welcome to Algonquin! May your trip to this incredible Park be an enjoyable one.

E VERY SEASON BRINGS new and dramatic changes to Algonquin. Both the landscape and the wildlife undergo spectacular transformations in the course of a year. Many of the phenomena for which the Park is famous demonstrate seasonal peaks in either activity or occurrence. By knowing the times of the year in which specific events occur, one can better plan a trip to coincide with some of those particular highlights (or, in the case of biting insects, to avoid them).

Each month is broken into three periods — early, middle and late. You might find that the symbol for "fair" activity (-) is located at the first of the month, the symbol for a higher level of activity [(o) for "good"] in the middle of the month, and the symbol representing the highest level of activity [(x) for "high"] at the end of the month. This simply indicates that your best chance of encountering this animal or phenomenon lies at the end of the month as opposed to the beginning of it. Some of the more frequently sought animals are illustrated here. While many are active year-round, there are particular times when they may be more easily viewed (or, as with wolves, more readily heard). Further information on specific animal activity throughout the seasons is found in **OBSERVING WILDLIFE**.

The blooming period of Park wildflowers stretches from mid-April to mid-September. However, different habitats produce distinct peaks in the flower cycles. In the hardwood forests the floor is carpeted with flowers in late April through to late May. This is the time when the forest floor is not yet shaded by overhead tree leaves. As soon as the canopy closes, these ephemerals vanish. A few shade-tolerant species such as Indian pipe bloom in summer shade. During summer a large variety of flowers flourish along the roadsides and other open sites where sunlight is unimpeded. For a photographic treatment of the various habitats and dominant flowers to be encountered in them, purchase the inexpensive Park publication *Wildflowers of Algonquin Provincial Park.*

May is the best month for viewing woodland flowers such as painted trillium.

Fall colours do peak at different times and with varying intensity from year to year, but generally the last week of September and the first week of October produce the best colours in the maples. However, once the maples have changed, other trees come into colour, with the deep yellow of poplars next in line. The view from the new Visitor Centre offers sensational displays of these trees. As time passes, the red oaks turn reddish-brown and can be seen on the hilltops throughout the Park, particularly on the East Side. Last, but not least, are the tamaracks or larches. These bog-loving trees are the only conifers to drop their needles. Before they lose them the trees turn an intense gold. Waterways through the Park simply blaze with this colour in late October.

If you wish to see colours at their peak, it is wise to call either the Visitor Centre or the information numbers to inquire about the status of the leaves. And, since snow conditions for skiing vary each year, you should call for information on the trails if you plan to do this activity near the extreme ends of the season.

One feature of Algonquin not illustrated on the following chart is the aurora borealis, otherwise known as the Northern Lights. Because the Park is situated on a high dome with no interference from city lights, the night sky is beautifully dark, which offers excellent stargazing opportunities as well as periodic views of the spectacular Northern Lights. The bizarre shimmering, at times colourful lights of the aurora are caused by interactions between the Earth's magnetic field and pockets of intensified magnetism in the sun's atmosphere. The aurora can be seen virtually any time of the year. Quite frequently it appears as a dull glow in the northern sky, while at other times pulsating rays shoot into the night. On other occasions vivid colours can be seen. Green is frequent, but vivid reds are also observed sometimes. In rare instances the colourful rays fill the entire sky in a cathedral effect, creating a mind-boggling display.

Key to Seasonal Chart

Code	Activity	Level of Activity
1	Otter	- Fair
2	Moose	o Good
3	Wildflowers	x High
4	Wolf Howling	
5	Beaver	
6	Biting Insects	
7	Fall Colours	
8	Ski / Snowshoe	

Seasonal Occurrences of a Few Algonquin Phenomena

	Jan	Feb	Mar	Apr	May	Jun	Jul	Aug	Sep	Oct	Nov	Dec
1	---	---	oox	xxx	o--	---	-oo	ooo	ooo	ooo	oo-	---
2	---	---	oox	xxx	xxx	xxx	xxx	ooo	ooo	ooo	ooo	---
3				-o	xxo	oox	xxx	oo-	-			
4	ooo	ooo	ooo	o--	---	---	oxx	xxx	xxx	xxo	ooo	ooo
5				--o	xxx	xxx	xxx	xxx	xxx	xxx	o-	
6				-	-ox	xxx	ooo	-				
7									-ox	xo-		
8	xxx	xxx	xo-									-ox

ALGONQUIN IS FAMOUS for its abundance and variety of wildlife, the result of the Park's mixture of southern and northern habitats. For many visitors the "must sees" include moose, Common Loons, beavers, Gray Jays, otters and timber wolves, although there is usually only a chance to hear the latter. Quite often Algonquin is the place where a person encounters these animals for the first time.

One frequently asked question is: "Are there any poisonous snakes in Algonquin Park?" Although Massasauga rattlesnakes, the only venomous reptiles in Ontario, are found west of the Park, unfortunately they are not known in Algonquin. I say unfortunately because it would be fantastic to have these rare and relatively harmless serpents as part of the fauna. The elevations that allow for the formation of boreal bogs are also responsible for the exclusion of many animals. Simply put, the Park is too cold for these fascinating, non-lethal reptiles.

As a rule, the animals we do have here are also harmless. Some people are concerned about black bears, but these mammals are normally extremely shy and usually very difficult to see. Timber wolves are almost impossible to spot and pose absolutely no threat to humans. The danger you face in driving to Algonquin far exceeds, by light-years, any danger posed by the natural inhabitants of the Park.

Although you can encounter many of Algonquin's animals by driving the roads or walking the trails, there are a few "tricks" that will substantially increase your chances of finding them during your visit to the Park. Since each species is usually located in a specific habitat at a certain time of the year, knowing the animal's life history will certainly aid you in your efforts. I highly recommend that you obtain the Algonquin Park publications on wildlife before your visit. These are inexpensive and do an excellent job of discussing the animals in terms of habitat preference. The appendix **IMPORTANT PUBLICATIONS** will provide the titles of these publications.

WILDLIFE-VIEWING ETIQUETTE

Before I begin to offer advice on how to find some of the Park's wildlife, I feel that it is absolutely essential that a short treatise on wildlife-viewing etiquette be given. Far too often during the excitement of seeing a wild animal up close for the first time, or while trying to get the ultimate photograph, the viewer's impact on the animal is overlooked. Algonquin's animals, no matter how tame they might appear to be, are indeed *wild* animals. Not only might a lack of consideration for the animal cause it unnecessary stress, it may also endanger yourself. Despite the obliviously contented look on the moose gleaning salt from the roadside ditch, that 450-kilogram (1,000-pound) animal can easily crush your skull with one kick of its great hoof. The most important rule to follow is: *Give all animals respect.* If a moose seems absurdly tame, why bother risking your life by testing its approachability to the limit? I'm not trying to create the impression that these animals are dangerous and one should be wary of them. Normally they are nonaggressive and one should never fear them. But how can we predict their behaviour if a crowd of 50 people begins to swarm around them? These creatures can certainly panic and might run through a group as easily as around it. If young are present, the mother might perceive a threat to her offspring and react instinctively and defensively. So play it safe by playing it smart. A few simple rules to follow are:

1. Never approach any wild animal too closely. Although it is impossible to provide *the* proper viewing distance, a general rule might be to stay back at least 20 metres from the larger animals.
2. Never lure animals onto roads where they might be hit by a vehicle, thereby endangering not only the animal but also the occupants of the vehicle.
3. Never harass wildlife by repeatedly playing recordings of their sounds in an effort to keep them close by or to attract them. If you are trying to get an owl, Spruce Grouse, moose or wolf to react to a recording, only play the tape a few times to get the animal's attention, then enjoy its response without further playbacks.
4. At night avoid shining powerful car-operated search beams into the eyes of animals. Some of these lights generate a tremendous glare that could damage the light-sensitive eyes of nocturnal animals.
5. Although feeding Gray Jays and chipmunks is acceptable, larger animals, particularly bears, should *never* be fed.
6. Do not disturb nesting birds, including loons. If these birds are repeatedly flushed out of their nests, odds are that the nesting attempt will fail.

WHEN AND HOW TO SEE WILDLIFE

For most wildlife the time of day is very important. Dusk arouses nocturnal animals; dawn initiates a flurry of activity in diurnal animals. Thus, the best time to look for animals is generally either the two or three hours following sunrise or the hour or two preceding sunset. I prefer the period from the predawn glow to about two hours after sunrise. Not only is this one of the best times to see wildlife, but it is also one of the most beautiful times of day. On cool mornings the heat of the sun warms your cheeks and also seems to penetrate your soul. In late summer spectacular mists shroud the waterways and other low places. At this time of day you feel a special closeness to the Park, a sensation that is difficult to put into words. And when you return to your breakfast table, the coffee, bacon and eggs taste extra good.

Since the behaviour of animals changes throughout the seasons, learning a bit about them before your visit might increase your chances of encountering them. For example, contrary to popular thinking, the best way to locate beavers is not to watch for them cutting down trees. During the summer in Algonquin, water plants form an important part of a beaver's diet. Therefore, the animal can usually be found by either watching for a V (the shape of the wake formed by a swimming beaver) cutting across the water or by scanning for a blunt-shaped head sticking up among the water-lilies.

Often an area that encompasses the borders of several different habitats might produce the largest variety of animals. Excursions to the edges of beaver ponds, swamps or larger bogs at the optimal times of day may reap the greatest rewards. You can enhance your viewing opportunities with a few simple tricks. If you are looking for birds, an easily produced series of sounds is almost guaranteed to draw them in for better viewing. Try making the sound *shhhhh,* then add a *p* to the front while doing so. The resulting noise is known as "pishing" or "spishing." By repeating *pshhhhh* in a short series (i.e., *pshhhhh, pshhhhh, pshhhhh, pshhhhh*), you should achieve amazing results. This call resembles the alarm calls of small birds and elicits a "mobbing" response in birds that hear it. Try "pishing" in quiet spots on trails or near forest edges. One word of warning, however. People who encounter you making that noise will inevitably be curious and yell, "What are you doing?" Never shout back, "Just pishing," or you might be misunderstood!

Another call that attracts larger birds, particularly hunters like owls or hawks, also serves to attract mammalian predators such as foxes, weasels (including martens and fishers), and occasionally even wolves. The sound is a squeal produced by noisily sucking on the knuckles of your index and middle fingers of one hand. When I lick my knuckles first, I find I achieve a better squeal. The resulting noise is similar to that of an injured prey and tends to draw the hunters in like steel to a magnet. Don't expect results every time, however. For this call to work the animal must be within earshot and must not have been alarmed by your presence.

Imitations of specific animal sounds will frequently entice the animals to respond and occasionally even appear. Perhaps the easiest animal to imitate is the timber wolf, and nothing is more rewarding than to be under a star-studded sky and have a wolf's spine-tingling howl shatter the silence in response to your rendition of its call. Because a human howl has the exact same qualities as that of a wild wolf, timber wolves readily answer a human imitation. Try giving a long howl that rises in the middle and drops at the end. Wait 10 to 15 seconds after an attempt before repeating it. I have found that if wolves respond it is usually after the second attempt. Sometimes, however, it takes several individual howls followed by a number of "group howls" (where one energetic person or two or three people simulate a pack by giving several consecutive howls each). An excellent explanation of howling is given in Algonquin Park Technical Bulletin No. 3, *Wolf Howling in Algonquin Provincial Park,* and superb recordings of wolves can be heard on the cassette *Voices of Algonquin.*

Wolves will answer all day, so try howling anytime, particularly if you find fresh tracks or droppings, especially those that are still steaming! At night, however,

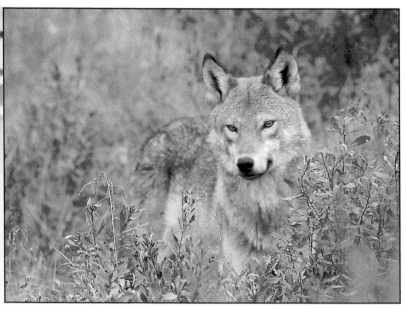

Timber wolves frequently howl in response to human imitations of their wild sounds.

sounds carry better, and with less bird, wind, leaf and traffic noise, distant sounds are more easily discerned. Large openings such as creeks, lake edges and bogs provide better long-range transmission of sound and are usually the best places to try.

Barred Owls are common throughout the Park and can often be stimulated into calling by imitations of their booming "who cooks for you, who cooks for you aaawwwll." Other loud noises, including wolf howls, may also elicit a response. *Voices of Algonquin* has superb recordings of this bird. It is noteworthy that imitations or tapes of this call in daytime attract a variety of birds, particularly woodpeckers such as Yellow-bellied Sapsuckers, Common Flickers, and the much sought after Black-backed Woodpecker. Before using a cassette, please read the section in this chapter called **Wildlife-viewing Etiquette.**

Otters are often seen on waterways throughout the Park. Frequently they respond to a snort and approach more closely. By blowing air through your mouth with your lips loosely flapping, an excellent rendition of an otter alarm call is produced. This sound will usually pique their curiosity and draw them in for better viewing.

The tremendous opportunity to view wild animals is indisputably one of the special features of Algonquin Park. Whether it be a chipmunk dominating a campground meal or a timber wolf howling into the night, these animals epitomize the untamed milieu for which the Park is famous. Please ensure that your enjoyment of these creatures does not have a detrimental effect either on them or on Algonquin.

PLATE 1
Tracks and Scats of Algonquin Large Mammals

MOOSE

summer

winter

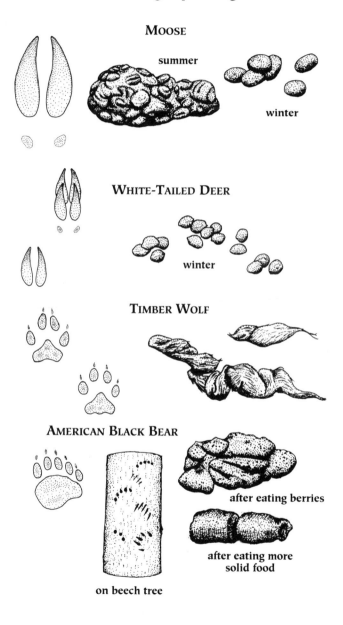

WHITE-TAILED DEER

winter

TIMBER WOLF

AMERICAN BLACK BEAR

after eating berries

after eating more
solid food

on beech tree

General Camping

THIS SECTION is designed to provide a few basic camping tips. Bill Mason's *Song of the Paddle* is an excellent reference for more detailed camping information.

Camping Etiquette

Algonquin is becoming an increasingly popular place for visitors to explore. Unfortunately there are always a few campers who are inconsiderate slobs by nature and tend to leave campsites, portages and trails in unsightly messes. This kind of user is virtually impossible to educate. However, sometimes an unthinking act is performed simply out of ignorance. It is these unconscious acts that might be reduced with a little bit of camping etiquette. Some general rules to follow are:

1. Never cut down live trees for firewood. Sufficient wood can always be gathered from fallen branches or dead trees. In the public campgrounds wood can be purchased. You can also bring your own supply to the drive-in campsites.
2. Use the provided facilities at campgrounds or campsites for your "washroom deposits." If you are in dire straits (for example, the "mood" strikes while on a trail or portage), then make sure you go off the trail and scrape a shallow depression into the ground. After completion of your duties, cover up all evidence with soil and leaves.
3. Never leave garbage at a site, thinking that someone else will pack it out for you. Pack out all items not

burnable. And remember, cans and bottles are pro-hibited in the Park Interior.

4. Use biodegradable soaps and shampoos on camping trips.

5. Never wash your dishes in lakes or rivers. Do this away from the water's edge.

6. Since sound travels so well at night, think of other campers when you feel moved to strike up a loud conversation or play a musical instrument. Be aware that radios, tape players and portable generators are not allowed in the Park Interior.

7. If possible, if you do encounter someone else's trash and you have room in your pack for it, consider carrying it out, as well.

8. Never start a fire outside of a designated fire pit and never leave a fire burning unattended.

Choosing a Site

Although camping in Algonquin can be broken down into two basic types, drive-in and Interior, there are site choices available for each. Along Highway 60 the campgrounds vary tremendously in available facilities as well as general environment. Too often a person grabs the first open campsite only to discover that another choice may have been preferable. If you are using a tent, never set it up in a depression. It can and certainly does rain in Algonquin, and low sites (as are frequently found in Lake of Two Rivers Campground) may fill up with water after a heavy rain. When choosing a site for a tent, try to select a slightly elevated, level area. If rain is anticipated, a heel-dug trench around the tent may help direct surface water away.

When tripping in the Interior, island campsites are preferred for a couple of reasons. As a rule, there is more wind and therefore fewer problems with biting insects. Also, islands frequently offer enhanced aesthetics in terms of sunrise and sunset viewing.

Remember, Interior camping may only be done at designated sites.

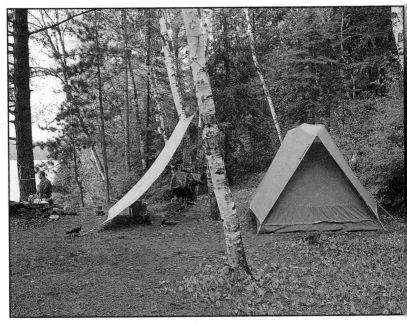

Algonquin offers superb wilderness camping experiences.

Equipment

Since an excellent treatment of camping equipment is covered in specific books, such as Bill Mason's *Song of the Paddle,* only a few tips are offered here.

A portable camp stove is a must for any camping trip. For drive-in camping larger multiburner stoves with big fuel tanks are commonly used. For Interior trips smaller single-burner backpacking stoves are preferred. The Coleman Peak series, MSR Whisperlite and Optimus stoves are a few examples. Remember that a camp stove is essential for any backpacking or canoeing trip, not only because of potential bad weather but also due to possible fire bans in the drier summer season.

For Interior camping no trip is complete without a good length of rope, toilet paper, a flashlight with new batteries, a first-aid kit, waterproof matches and either a *Canoe Routes of Algonquin Provincial Park* or a *Backpacking Trails of Algonquin Provincial Park* map brochure. Ziploc bags seem to have been invented for Interior tripping, since they can be used to keep maps, toilet paper and food dry. Although waterproof matches can be purchased, I still place these (along with their striking pad) and regular strike-anywhere matches in airtight containers. Formerly I used 35 mm film canisters for holding matches and spices but have now discovered a far superior container — urine-sample bottles, the kind common in medical clinics. These bottles are great for camping trips: they are extremely lightweight and also *very* waterproof. But just in case you are wondering, I only use new bottles.

Even though a light camping axe can be a useful piece of equipment, I often go on shorter trips without one. A folding saw, such as a Sven, is lighter to pack, occupies less space than an axe and is also more practical. Since the bulk of firewood used is generally branch-sized, the saw is all you need to cut up wood. For more extended trips I pack both a saw and an axe. After a day or two of hard rain, much of the smaller wood gets soaked, so I use my saw to cut up small blocks from larger fallen trunks, then split them with the axe to get at the drier wood inside.

When on an Interior trip, one very important rule is to keep matches and your sleeping bag free of moisture. While many of the sleeping bag sacks are reasonably waterproof, I still put my sleeping bag in a garbage bag to ensure dryness.

The One-match Fire

Whether you are camping in a public campground along the highway or on a remote island reached after a day's paddle by canoe, the mechanics of successfully starting a campfire are the same. Too often an attempt is made to ignite chunks of wood the size of a tree trunk. The best strategy is to start small and only add larger pieces of wood after the fire is established. In fact, many cooking fires only require wood the thickness of a pencil.

Fires must be set only inside the pit located at every designated camping spot. If the pit is full of loose ash from previous fires, clean it out before you prepare your fuel. Prior to constructing your fire, make sure that adequate fuel has been collected. If you are in a public campground, wood is sold at designated places and times. *Never* cut down living trees or strip bark or branches from them. Even the most heavily used Interior sites will have sufficient starting fuel near the fire pit.

Start off with a base of loose, easily ignited material. If you have waste paper with you, that will suffice. I find that small strips of white birch bark, which can usually be found lying on the ground or can be taken from logs or dead trees, works extremely well. If neither is available, dry pine needles and/or knife shavings from a dry stick will do. Next, add fine twigs, or "twiglets," as I call them. The best kind to use are the very fine dead twigs found on the bottom branches of coniferous trees such as spruce and balsam fir. These are also usually scattered on the ground. If you are in a campground, use an axe to slice off thin slivers of wood, otherwise known as "kindling." A couple of handfuls should be enough. On top of this add larger twigs and small branches (or larger kindling if at a campground), forming a rough pyramid. Now strike a match and light the base. Unless you are making an evening's-end fire, the largest wood pieces required should be the same size as the last ones you added to this fuel pile.

If a strong wind is blowing, build a windbreak out of stones. A strategically placed backpack will also help reduce the effect of the breeze. Never build a large fire under windy conditions. The camp stove should be used when cooking under these conditions.

When it comes time to call it a day, be sure to put out your fire. While it may be calm when you retire to the tent, a wind could easily spring up overnight. Also, never leave a site while a fire is still burning or the coals are still glowing, and thoroughly dowse the pit with water to ensure no accidents happen.

Wood can be purchased at the drive-in campgrounds, but there is nothing wrong with bringing your own supply.

Food

Perhaps the most important rule is never to have a messy campsite. Food scraps, dirty dishes, exposed food and even coolers left lying around serve to attract a variety of animals, including black bears. If you are staying in a drive-in campground, place all waste material in the bearproof garbage structures. Never bring food into your tent; the odours will linger, possibly attracting a hungry scavenger. Make sure food is not left on the tables and that coolers are stored in your vehicle trunk overnight or when you are away from the site. If you are staying at an Interior site, burn all burnable leftovers and place nonburnables with your food in a pack hung well off the ground.

I usually bring at least one 10-metre rope on all Interior trips. Pines with a stout lower limb projecting from the trunk at least four metres above the ground are ideal for hanging packs. If you have difficulty throwing the rope over a branch, try weighting it with a piece of wood or a stone.

Sometimes two ropes are necessary if a suitable tree can't be found. You can tie one length between two adjacent trees, then the other piece over the first one. However, single trees are far simpler for hanging packs, and a bit of searching near the site will usually turn one up.

The pack should be hung at least three metres (nine feet) off the ground and at least one metre (three feet) from the trunk. *Never* leave your food in a pack on the ground, in the canoe or in the tent overnight or when you are away from the campsite.

The type of food a person brings to the Park depends primarily on the type of camping one does. Drive-in campgrounds allow the visitor to bring virtually any type of food. Canoeists and backpackers must carry lighter and less easily spoiled foods. Excellent suggestions for suitable foods to bring can be found on the back of the *Canoe Routes of Algonquin Provincial Park* map brochure, the essential publication for any Park canoe trip, and Bill Mason's *Song of the Paddle*.

When walking trails exceeding two kilometres in length, it may be wise to bring food and beverages to get you through the trip.

Water

Drive-in campgrounds have treated water available. For Interior trips water must be used from untreated sources. Many users, including myself, drink water from larger lakes untreated. This practice is generally safe if water is taken away from the shore and down as far as the hand can reach. However, there is always a remote chance of contacting giardia or "beaver fever" by drinking untreated water, so many campers use either filtration systems or purification tablets available at any camping or outfitting store.

Boiling the water will also make it potable but, unfortunately, if you want a cool drink, you have to wait quite a while. Backpackers should carry water with them, replenishing reserves if necessary when lakes are encountered. Regardless of where you are in the Park, never drink untreated water from beaver ponds or bogs.

Clothing

Because of Algonquin's elevations the nights can be surprisingly cool, even cold, in late spring and mid-summer. The best strategy if you are camping in drive-in locations is to bring a heavy sweater or jacket, perhaps even a light parka, especially in August. If you are camping in the Interior, then several layers of clothes are preferable to a heavy parka. Layers of loose clothes tend to be warmer (each layer traps air) than one heavy garment. A T-shirt, a long-sleeved cotton shirt, a light sweater and a windbreaker should do quite nicely. The beauty of layering is that you can mix and match to suit the temperatures. Be sure to bring rainwear no matter where or when you are camping, otherwise you may be confined to either wearing wet clothes or staying inside the tent until the rain ends, which might be several days. One important consideration is colour. During fly season (see **Biting Insects** in this chapter), light colours such as tan or pale yellow are much better than dark colours, especially blue or black.

Footwear should consist of shoes with good treads for walking trails or portages. Although hiking boots might seem ideal for Algonquin, as far as most people are concerned, including myself, they are not necessary. Comfortable hiking shoes or good running shoes normally suffice. The important thing is to bring a spare pair in case one pair gets wet. If you have weak ankles and are concerned about sprains, then hiking boots might offer better support. However, travelling along an Algonquin trail is not like climbing the Rocky Mountains, although the Centennial Ridges Trail might be the exception!

OTHER TIPS

The following will cover a few more general pieces of advice for Park users.

Biting Insects

The main challenge when camping in Algonquin at certain times of the year is dealing with biting insects. The good news is that each insect has its own particular season. The bad news is that the seasons tend to merge, producing a prolonged period of bloodletting. However, different people respond to each type of insect differently, and there are ways of reducing your attractiveness to these biting terrors.

First, let's meet the little devils. Black flies are among the smaller biting flies in Algonquin. Since they lay their eggs on rocks in fast-flowing, cold streams, Algonquin is perfect for a number of species to call home. The majority of those that bite emerge as adults from these cold waters in spring, usually anywhere from mid-May to mid-June. However, during an early spring they might venture out in late April, and some years they persist well into July.

For those who have never met the black fly, you will be amazed at how such a tiny creature can make life so miserable. Black flies are active on warm days, particularly in the evening, but desist when the sun sets. Like most biting flies, it is only the female that bites, seeking a blood meal for her developing eggs. However, black flies tend to tear rather than bite flesh. Blood, induced by anticoagulants injected into the wounds, copiously flows from the small gashes. Just like sharks drawn to a bloodbath, seeming thousands soon attack in a relentless and furious feeding frenzy.

Mosquitoes are the next most common type of biting insect in Algonquin. Although these creatures have a much longer flying season than black flies (they tend to appear by late May and some species remain active into the middle of August), they are rarely as bothersome as their smaller brethren. Of course, this is all very subjective; some people find a couple of mosquitoes totally unbearable. Mosquitoes tend to dominate the last hour or so of the day but can also be encountered while prowling around moist woods. Any portage through rich hardwoods or low areas will inevitably produce a hungry swarm.

By midsummer another "nasty" creature appears. Deer flies are larger flies with banded wings and gorgeous eyes (usually red or green). Their most common point of attack is your head, which they love to buzz around. Horse flies are a larger relative of deer flies. Both types of flies impart a nasty burning prick when they "let you have it."

One last type of fly that you might encounter in summer, particularly along waterways, is the stable fly. These house-fly-sized insects have the annoying habit of biting your ankles when you are canoeing and are very adept at escaping your swat no matter how fast you might be.

With all that said what can possibly be done apart from visiting the Park at another time of year, say, December? Well, there are actually a few things you can do to lessen the annoyance these small but at times dominant animals might cause you.

A number of effective insect repellents are available on the market. Since biting insects tend to home in on water vapour gradients next to your skin, the drying effects of these repellents tend to disrupt the insect's detection systems. Many types contain the active ingredient DEET. While these repellents work quite well for many people, I can't tell you which types work the best for the simple reason that I don't use them. I dislike the "meltdown" effect most brands have on binoculars and camera equipment. Some types lack DEET in their constitution and have components such as citronella instead. These may be an alternative for those who find the first chemical unpleasant.

Clothing selection is certainly important in insect avoidance. Many biting insects are attracted to dark colours, particularly dark blue and black. Lighter colours such as pale yellow or light tans will help you avoid the biting clouds. I will never forget paddling by a campsite one evening in early June. On the point stood a forlorn-looking woman, dressed in black pants and a black top and sporting a black hat. This was at the height of the black fly season, and her face and neck were a mass of open bleeding wounds from the fly bites. Although I wasn't enjoying the company of the flies swarming around me, I only bore a couple of bites on my exposed flesh.

Besides being light in colour, clothing should be loose-fitting with tight cuffs. I close all buttons and raise the collar. Usually I wear a light-coloured jacket over the shirt. A hat is essential to keep the pests out of your hair. Flies love tender ankles for dessert, so a pair of heavier socks pulled over your pant legs will protect these body parts. I must admit this sort of outfit tends to look silly, but believe me, in Algonquin during the height of fly season, fashion-wise clothes are as useless as high heels on the Centennial Ridges Trail.

Another trick I find to be quite successful is one that is also a little embarrassing to share with you. Perfumes in soaps and shampoos seem to attract insects, as do open pores from frequent bathing. If I am camping or taking photographs during peak fly season, I tend to bathe very irregularly. When I absolutely must clean myself, I avoid using soap of any type. There is a definite inverse relationship between the number of flies that bite you and the number of days since your last bath. Also, I wear the same clothes for as long as possible without washing them. Although these are excellent ways of reducing the number of biting flies, you won't win any friends.

Last but not least there are some excellent bugproof clothes on the market, including the traditional netted "bug hat," which might make you look like something from outer space. Then there are "bug jackets" that keep insects away from your body. Some of these must be dipped in the noxious repellents before they work. However, one type sold by most outfitters is an exception. Its elasticized cuffs and drawstring waist protect you from insects. The hood has a mesh face guard and can be unzipped at the neck to free your head. The best one I have tried is the Original Bug Shirt, which is made of lightweight tan cotton and has vents to prevent sweating. In the ultimate test I sat next to a beaver pond at the height of black fly season for several hours in the evening with this jacket on. I was amazed that none of the 2,989 black flies swarming outside this barrier were able to get in. I was also pleased that I could see well enough through the mesh to focus my camera without unfastening the hood.

Whatever method you use to combat biting insects there are always some inherent drawbacks. However, you will find the more you expose yourself to insects the less bothersome they are. If you are severely affected by their bites, as some people are, I would recommend that you come to Algonquin during the off-season for flies. Usually the period from mid-August to late September is free of these insects, and at this time the temperatures are quite pleasant for sleeping in a tent.

Poisonous Snakes, Mushrooms and Poison Ivy

Campers are frequently concerned about poisonous plants and animals. Once again, there are no poisonous snakes in Algonquin. Nor is there poison ivy along the Highway Corridor, although immature sarsaparilla is often mistaken for this irritating plant. On the other hand, poison ivy is occasionally encountered north of the Corridor and is relatively common along rivers in the eastern part of the Park.

There are a few poisonous mushrooms so, unless you are quite familiar with this type of fungi, avoid eating any during your visit. *Mushrooms of Algonquin Provincial Park* is an excellent publication for those seeking more information.

Walking the Trails

Since most of the interpretive trails are short, no special advice is needed for them. However, some of the trails, notably Mizzy Lake, Track and Tower and Centennial Ridges, are longer and require more time to complete. To avoid running into difficulty I recommend starting the trail early in the morning as opposed to late afternoon. If you are inclined to start a longer trail later in the day, bring a flashlight.

It is also prudent to carry a small daypack with a bit of nourishment, such as trail mix or fruit, and some type of beverage in a container that will return with you. It can get quite hot in summer, and on most of the longer trails you will come across a few hills.

It is always an excellent idea to bring along some toilet paper or Kleenex. One never knows when "nature will call." Be sure to be discreet. Walk well off the trail, deposit "the goods" in a depression and cover up the "dirty deed" with leaves and soil once you are finished.

Plate 2
Some Common Algonquin Conifers

Balsam Fir

White Spruce

Black Spruce

Tamarack

Eastern Hemlock

Jack Pine

Red Pine

White Pine

5 The Highway 60 Corridor

THE MOST POPULAR ROUTE into Algonquin is Highway 60. Along the Highway Corridor are situated the majority of the Park's campgrounds, interpretive trails and facilities, as well as other services. Despite the developed aspect and prominent use of this part of Algonquin, it is still possible to feel as though you are really "back in the woods" and have bona fide wilderness experiences. Also, wildlife-viewing opportunities in the Corridor are equal to, in some cases better than, those off the road in the Park Interior.

Information and permits, which every vehicle must display, are available at both the East and West gates. The East Gate is easily located because you must pass through a set of arches when you reach it. The Information Building is accessed from the right lane. The West Gate entrance has been modified in recent years so that you might conceivably pass it if distracted. After you reach the western boundary of Algonquin (identified by a sign on your right side), the West Gate lies four kilometres ahead. Watch for the right-turning lane that enters the parking area adjacent to the West Gate office. Remember, you must have a permit whether you are in the Park for a half day or a week. Only people just passing through the Park (i.e., not using Park facilities) are not required to buy a permit.

Reflective signs, frequently situated on telephone posts, indicate the distance in kilometres from the West Gate. Throughout the Park literature locations of points of interest are defined using these kilometre markers.

The Highway 60 Corridor is one of the most popular access points.

For example, the Western Uplands Backpacking Trail is located three kilometres east of the West Gate at the kilometre 3 (KM 3) sign, and the Bat Lake Trail is at kilometre 30 (KM 30), 30 kilometres east of the West Gate. The same system will be used in this book when describing locations along the Corridor. The distance between markers will be used for more precise location descriptions. For example, the Mizzy Lake Trail entrance is situated 0.4 kilometre east of the kilometre 15 (KM 15) marker. Thus, its location would be given as KM 15.4.

An excellent summary of the current Corridor facilities and activities can be found in the free tabloid *Algonquin Provincial Park: The Parkway Corridor*, available at most Park offices or upon request by mail or phone.

THE ALGONQUIN VISITOR CENTRE — KM 43

A major project undertaken for the Park centennial in 1993, the Algonquin Visitor Centre is without question one of the finest interpretive centres in Canada. Every aspect of this incredible showpiece, including the breathtaking location, is simply spectacular.

The first section of the display area illustrates how the Park's topography has affected the present-day composition of flora and fauna by its influence on climate and soils. The next gallery depicts through stunning dioramas all of the Park's major habitats, from spruce bog to hardwood forest, from lake to coniferous forest. The array of animals in the dioramas ranges from tiny shrews to massive moose. The animals are situated in realistic surroundings with painted backdrops that can only be described as genuine works of art. Whether it be the beaver pond diorama complete with dam, pond and lodge, or the bear exhibit with a mother bear tearing apart a log while her cub looks on with curiosity, the realism is incredible.

The human history level profiles man's involvement in Algonquin. Exhibits profile various people, ranging from early inhabitants to more recent residents, such as the famous artist Tom Thomson, and discuss their involvement and impact on the Park. A comfortable theatre offers programs that further explain the past and present features of Algonquin.

The dioramas, displays and programs have all been designed to provide visitors with an understanding of the complexity of the Park. Visitors are now better prepared to appreciate the "real thing," which is gloriously on display from a partially enclosed viewing deck. The deck overlooks a spectacular vista encompassing a sweeping bog, rolling hardwood hills, two lakes and a boreal forest — the very subjects explained throughout the displays inside. The view alone is worth the trip. Occasionally animals such as

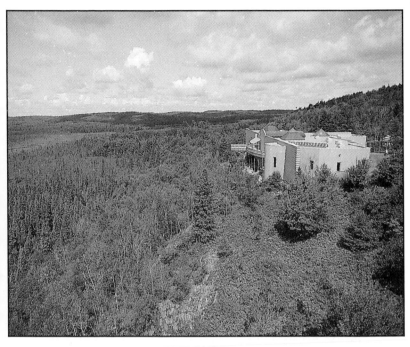

The Algonquin Visitor Centre, a major project for the Park centennial, offers a spectacular view.

moose and wolves are seen or heard from this wonderful vantage point.

The Visitor Centre also contains a restaurant and an excellent bookstore, as well as a room for temporary exhibits. The Centre is open seven days a week for most of the year (in winter it may be open only weekends). Be sure to set aside part of a day to visit this amazing addition to the Park.

THE ALGONQUIN LOGGING MUSEUM — KM 54.6

This outdoor museum offers a fascinating look at an important aspect of Algonquin's history. The log Reception Building houses an information desk, bookstore and theatre. An audiovisual program provides an overview of the logging history of the Park, and a

35

delightful trail complete with guidebook starts from the Reception Building and leads through the outdoor exhibits. These include a replica of an early camboose camp and one of the last remaining alligators, a steam-driven paddle boat that could also be winched across land. Around the turn of the century it was used for towing log booms. Appropriately this unique exhibit rests beside a scenic pond created by a replicated log dam. A log chute, similar to the ones used to transport logs around waterfalls and rapids, bypasses the small rapids below the dam.

The outdoor exhibits are strategically located along this trail in a chronological sequence, which allows the visitor to see how logging has changed over the past 150 years. The Algonquin Logging Museum is open from late May until Thanksgiving weekend.

THE INTERPRETIVE WALKING TRAILS

One of the most appealing features of the Highway 60 Corridor is the variety of superb interpretive walking trails. There are 13 distinctly different trails, each offering unique insights into the Park's habitats and intriguing history. An inexpensive (37 cents in 1992!) illustrated trail guide is available at the start of each trail or at retail outlets in the Park. These booklets contain text that is read at corresponding numbered posts along the trail, allowing you to learn firsthand and at your own leisure about Algonquin's many facets.

The following is a brief synopsis of the different trails. The highway location follows the name of the trail. A brief overview of the trail is then provided and the trail length appears in brackets at the end of the description.

Whiskey Rapids Trail — KM 7.2

This trail follows the scenic Oxtongue River, and the trail guide explores the ecology of the river (2.1 kilometres).

Hardwood Lookout Trail — KM 13.8

This short trail brings you through a beautiful hardwood forest, while the trail guide explores its ecology. Scenic views of the Smoke Lake area and a side trail to a stand of red spruce, a relatively rare tree, are highlights (0.8 kilometre).

Mizzy Lake Trail — KM 15.4

This, the second longest trail, is well worth the effort because it passes through some outstanding wildlife-viewing areas, particularly in the northern part. A total of nine small lakes and ponds are visited, and the wildlife they support is highlighted in the trail guide (11 kilometres).

Peck Lake Trail — KM 19.2

The ecology of very pretty Peck Lake is the focus of this trail, which meanders around the lake periphery through a delightful coniferous forest (1.9 kilometres).

Track and Tower Trail — KM 25

This popular trail explores some of the fascinating history of Algonquin. It travels through some extensive hardwood forests and crosses many pretty streams. The historic landmarks include remnants of several OA & PS Railway trestles and the site of a former fire lookout tower with a spectacular view over Cache Lake. Part of the trail lies on the old railway bed of the OA & PS Railway. The Track and Tower Trail can also be reached from Mew Lake (7.7 kilometres with an optional 5.5-kilometre loop from Mew Lake Campground).

Hemlock Bluff Trail — KM 27.2

This trail first leads through a grove of towering hemlocks and later visits a cliff overlooking Jack Lake. Research in Algonquin is the topic examined in the trail guide (3.5 kilometres).

Bat Lake Trail — KM 30

This trail is relatively easy to walk despite its length. It passes through a younger mixed forest, enters an exceptionally large hemlock grove, traverses a bog and visits a fine lookout as well as a naturally acidified lake. The trail guide examines basic ecological principles (5.6 kilometres).

Two Rivers Trail — KM 31

A fine view from a cliff top is the highlight of this trail, which wanders through a younger Algonquin forest. The dynamics of forest change are explored (2.1 kilometres).

Centennial Ridges Trail — two kilometres south from KM 37.6

The newest of the Corridor trails, it gets its name from its year of opening — 1993, the Park centennial. It is the most rugged of all the highway trails, but the hike is worth the effort. Some of the finest views in the Park are found atop the two ridges the trail visits. The trail guide details contributions made by famous Park personalities (10 kilometres).

Lookout Trail — KM 39.7

One of the most spectacular of all the trails, Lookout Trail holds true to its name and visits a cliff offering a breathtaking view. The trail guide explores the geology of Algonquin. On the rather steep climb to the top (which means a downhill walk on the return) one encounters interesting features, including a glacial erratic (a glacier-moved rock) as big as a mobile home (1.9 kilometres).

Booth's Rock Trail — 9 kilometres south from KM 40.3

Another spectacular view is offered from this trail, which also visits two small lakes. After visiting the ruins of the Barclay Estate, you return on the old railway bed. Man's impact on Algonquin is the theme of the trail guide (5.1 kilometres).

Spruce Bog Boardwalk — KM 42.5

This short trail is not only one of the most unique but also one of the easiest to walk. The fascinating ecology of a northern bog is explored as you travel through and over the Sunday Creek bog on boardwalks. Northern flora and fauna highlight this trail (1.5 kilometres).

Beaver Pond Trail — KM 45.2

One of my favourites, this trail visits two beaver ponds and allows you to explore the ecology of this common Park mammal. Certainly one of the better wildlife-viewing trails (2.0 kilometres).

BIKE TRAILS

At the time of writing only one mountain bike trail exists along the Corridor. The Minnesing Mountain Bike Trail, at KM 23, occupies the Minnesing Cross-country Ski Trail. The 23 kilometres of trail traverse a variety of terrain and offer varying degrees of physical challenge, some sections more so than others.

A second bike trail will open sometime in the future. It will follow the old railway bed of the OA & PS Railway between Lake of Two Rivers and Rock Lake. This trail will offer 10 kilometres of hard-surfaced trail and will be ideal for family outings.

BACKPACKING TRAILS

Two excellent backpacking trails can be reached from the Highway Corridor. While both offer loops that can be walked in one full day (if you are in good shape and are an accomplished hiker), these trails are primarily designed for overnight use. The regulations for the Interior apply to users of this trail. Refer to **OTHER ACCESS POINTS** for details on these rules.

Backpacking Trails of Algonquin Provincial Park provides detailed maps and information concerning these trails. It is available from The Friends of Algonquin Park (address provided in the appendix **IMPORTANT SER-VICES**) or from the gates.

The Western Uplands Backpacking Trail — KM 3

This is the longest backpacking trail in the Park and offers loops ranging from 32 to 88 kilometres. Access to this trail is also achieved from the Rain Lake Access, providing backpackers with the option of hiking the trail from Highway 60 to Rain Lake, or vice versa, without returning. As its name suggests, this trail travels through typical West Side hardwood uplands.

Highland Backpacking Trail — KM 29.7

This trail offers loops of 19 and 35 kilometres. The short loop encircles Provoking Lake while the longer loop also visits Head and Harness lakes.

CROSS-COUNTRY SKI TRAILS

During winter Algonquin is enveloped by a silent beauty not found at other times of the year. Three excellent cross-country trails allow skiers to explore the Park during this invigorating season. All the trails have shelters (many with heat available) and emergency barrels (each containing a first-aid kit, spare ski tip, roll of duct tape, matches, fire starter, kindling, candles, an emergency blanket, sleeping bag and chocolate bars) at points along their lengths. Each trail is packed and groomed, and track-setting occurs whenever weather conditions and manpower permit. Various levels of challenge are offered and identified on each trail.

Currently, on weekends during the ski season, skis, snowshoes, winter sleeping bags and tents are available for rent at the West Gate. If you intend to use this service, be sure to check with the Park and confirm its operation. The free brochure *Algonquin Provincial Park in Winter* details these trails and supplies general winter regulations and tips. It is available at the gates or the Park Information Office.

Fen Lake Trail — starts at West Gate

This trail offers loops of 1.25, 5.2 and 13 kilometres. Much of the trail passes through typical West Side hardwood forest.

Minnesing Trail — KM 23

The return section of the trail follows the historic Minnesing Road which, in early years, carried visitors from the railway station at Cache Lake to the Minnesing Lodge on Burnt Island Lake. A variety of loops, varying from 4.7 to 23.4 kilometres, offer skiers a number of options. The trail traverses a variety of terrain, and spectacular scenery is a feature over much of its length.

Leaf Lake Trail — KM 53.9

This is one of the favourite trails of Algonquin skiers. A large number of habitats and spectacular vistas are seen. Several loops allow for a variety of distances to be covered during the outing. Here one can ski as little as five or as many as 17 kilometres of trail.

PICNIC GROUNDS

Seven picnic grounds are situated along the Corridor. In order of appearance from west to east these are Oxtongue River (KM 3), Tea Lake Dam (KM 8.1), Hardwood Hill (KM 16.7), Little Madawaska (KM 21.4), Lake of Two Rivers (KM 33.8), Lake of Two Rivers East (KM 35.4) and Costello Creek (KM 46.3). While all are kept clean and have outdoor washrooms, there are several that are more aesthetically pleasing because they are situated on water. Perhaps the prettiest of all is the Tea Lake Dam Picnic Ground, found on the picturesque Oxtongue River. The Lake of Two Rivers sites are also quite nice thanks to their location on a large, scenic lake with good beaches within easy access of the picnic sites. In addition to these official picnic grounds, picnic tables are also located at Canisbay

Lake (north from KM 23.1), at KM 23.3 (north side of the highway) and at the Lake of Two Rivers Store (KM 31.4).

RESTAURANTS AND LODGES

Meals can be purchased along the highway at several locations. Generally the restaurants don't open until May and are usually open until Thanksgiving, except for the Visitor Centre restaurant, which might offer coffee and muffins in winter. It is best to check in advance if you visit in the off-season and wish to eat in Park facilities. Your needs and budget will be considerations when choosing a place to eat inside the Park. The three lodges that serve meals to the general public as well as to their guests tend to be considerably more expensive, since they offer more elaborate meals. You may wish to inquire about prices before committing yourself. Of course, numerous restaurants are situated outside the Park and are open year-round.

All three lodges offer accommodation throughout most of the usual visitation season. Only Bartlett Lodge on Cache Lake offers accommodation in winter. Since this may change on a yearly basis, be sure to inquire before planning to stay there. Dates of operation and prices can be acquired by phone or letter, and addresses are provided in the appendix **IMPORTANT SERVICES**.

- The Portage Store (KM 14.1) offers light meals and the restaurant overlooks Canoe Lake.
- Arowhon Pines Lodge (eight kilometres north from KM 15.4) offers full-course meals. It is best to reserve by phone (705-633-5661/5662).
- Bartlett Lodge (on Cache Lake, south from KM 23.5) is accessible by water only (a boat will taxi you to the lodge) and offers full-course meals. It is best to reserve by phone (705-633-5543).
- Lake of Two Rivers Store (KM 31.4) has a restaurant specializing in take-out fast food, and it also has a small sit-down section.

- Killarney Lodge (KM 33.2) offers full meal services, but it may be best to phone in advance (705-633-5551).
- The Algonquin Visitor Centre (KM 43) has a restaurant offering not only a variety of snacks and light meals but also a spectacular view from the dining area.

STORES

Three stores are situated along the Highway Corridor. The Portage Store on Canoe Lake (KM 14.1) has a souvenir shop adjoining the restaurant, and a complete outfitting store is situated on the lower level. This is the only location in the Park where gasoline is available. The Lake of Two Rivers Store (KM 31.4) offers a variety of groceries and personal essentials as well as souvenirs. The Opeongo Store (north from KM 46.3) is primarily an outfitting store but does offer a small selection of drinks and camping foods. Some souvenirs are also available here.

BOOKSTORES

A superb bookstore operated by a cooperating association, The Friends of Algonquin Park, is located at the Algonquin Visitor Centre (KM 43). Publications specifically dealing with the Park are sold here as well as an excellent selection of natural history, human history and children's books.

The Friends also operate a smaller bookstore at the Algonquin Logging Museum (KM 54.6). In addition, all the stores in the Park offer a small selection of publications. Park publications are also available at both gates.

CAMPGROUNDS

Nine campgrounds are situated in the Corridor. These vary tremendously in size, atmosphere and facilities. None have electrical outlets at the individual campsites. However, Canisbay (KM 23.1), Mew Lake (KM 30.6), Lake of Two Rivers (KM 31.8), Kearney Lake

(KM 36.5) and Pog Lake (KM 36.9) all have flush toilets and showers. Of these, all but Kearney also have laundry facilities. Rock Lake (eight kilometres south from KM 40.3), Lake of Two Rivers and Tea Lake (KM 11.4) are the only campgrounds where motorboats with up to 20-horsepower motors are allowed on the lake. Most campgrounds have good beaches except Tea Lake and Coon Lake (south from KM 40.3). Lake of Two Rivers and Mew Lake are within walking distance of the Lake of Two Rivers Store, but that also means these campgrounds are more exposed to highway noise. The ninth campground, Whitefish Lake Group Campground, is available for organized groups on a reservation basis only.

If privacy is your main concern, then I recommend Canisbay as the best and Pog Lake second best. Canisbay is situated in a beautiful hardwood forest with relatively isolated sites. Pog Lake lies in a plantation-style pinewoods and has many waterfront sites. Both campgrounds have sections that are well distanced from highway noise. Rock Lake and Lake of Two Rivers have the least isolated campsites and may be noisier than other campgrounds during the busy period (mid-July to mid-August). Obviously the type of facilities available and the degree of privacy offered are important factors to consider when choosing a campground.

All campgrounds are open from late June until Labour Day. Rock Lake, Lake of Two Rivers and Tea Lake open in May and close in October. Mew Lake is the only campground that offers winter camping.

Firewood is sold at wood yards in Mew and Pog Lake campgrounds, and at the Rock Lake office. During fall and winter, wood is available at Mew Lake.

Canisbay has an additional feature that other campgrounds lack. Campsites situated at the north end of the lake can only be reached by canoe. These are known as "paddle-in sites" and offer users a taste of Interior camping.

Each campground has its own pamphlet complete with map of the sites. Reserved sites are available at Mew Lake, Lake of Two Rivers, Pog Lake and Canisbay campgrounds. The reservation number is 705-633-5538/5725 and the Park information number is 705-633-5572.

THE INTERPRETIVE PROGRAM

Algonquin has one of the finest interpretive programs in North America. Programs, held daily from late June until Labour Day, consist of Conducted Walks as well as Children's and Evening Programs.

The Conducted Walks are usually a leisurely hour and a half long and focus on specific subjects such as birds, wildflowers, insects, mushrooms, trees and forest ecology. In addition, slightly longer outings explore wildlife habitats at special times of the day. Evening Walks visit excellent habitats for beaver, moose and otter. Night Walks explore the nocturnal activity along a quiet trail, and the wild calls of Barred Owls are frequently a highlight. Canoe Outings are half-day events that explore aquatic habitats as well as provide some canoe tripping tips.

Algonquin for Kids focuses on the younger audience and deals with topics ranging from reptiles and amphibians to animal defences. These programs are held at the Algonquin Visitor Centre.

Evening Programs are held every night at the Outdoor Theatre (KM 35.4). They usually last about an hour and a half and consist of two films and a slide presentation. Topics include birds, reptiles and amphibians, beavers, wolves, moose, lakes and fishing, wildflowers, Tom Thomson and canoe tripping. In bad weather the programs are held inside the Visitor Centre.

Public Wolf Howls are held on Thursdays in August if wolves and weather permit. At these immensely popular events participants first attend a talk on wolves and wolf howling at the Outdoor Theatre. Then they are taken to a site where naturalists attempt to elicit responses from wild wolves by giving vocal imitations of their howls.

In recent years the interpretive program has been offered on weekends between Labour Day and Thanksgiving. Evening Programs are performed indoors, but walks are still held outdoors.

All of the locations, times and themes of the events are provided in the weekly flyer *This Week in Algonquin*. This is available in dispensers and posted on bulletin boards throughout the Park. A special autumn edition lists all the events when fall programming is available.

The naturalist staff, both seasonal and permanent, is of the highest calibre. They are always more than willing to answer any questions concerning the Park's flora, fauna or history. If you would like something identified or desire information on any particular aspect of Algonquin, feel free to inquire at the Visitor Centre.

WILDLIFE-VIEWING AREAS

Many of the interpretive trails and outings offer excellent opportunities to encounter some of the Park's famed wildlife. Perhaps the two finest trails for general wildlife viewing are Beaver Pond and Mizzy Lake. Each offers a mixture of habitats, including ponds supporting active beaver colonies and superb summer moose-feeding sites. Wolves also frequent these areas in some years, particularly late summer. In fact, Wolf Howl Pond on the Mizzy Lake Trail is so named because timber wolves are commonly heard howling from the boggy meadows at the northwest end of the pond. Otters are also frequently seen, particularly in the waterways along the Mizzy Trail.

If encountering wildlife is one of the goals of your trip, refer to **OBSERVING WILDLIFE** for tips and advice on general wildlife viewing. Many of the species can be attracted with specific calls and noises, and these are outlined in this section. In Chapter 3 **Wildlife-viewing Etiquette** offers recommendations on how to avoid disturbing the animals while you are viewing them.

The following is a discussion of sites for some of the more popular species. For simplicity these suggested sites are listed starting from the west side.

Moose

The Highway Corridor can be as good as, at times perhaps even better than, the Interior for seeing this great monarch of the north. During the winter, moose lack sodium, an essential mineral, in their diet. By spring they are sodium-starved. A number of moose discover that the roadside ditches are enriched with sodium in the form of salt from winter road maintenance. Numbers of moose can be readily viewed from April through June along the highway, gleaning salt from the muddy ditches and puddles.

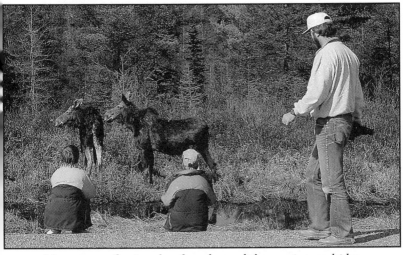

Moose are easily viewed as they glean salt from spring roadsides.

From June through to late July moose get their natural source of sodium from water plants, particularly water-shield (*Brasenia schreberi*). A number of lakes, ponds and streams along the highway edge offer good viewing opportunities, particularly in the evening.

I recommend checking the pond across from the Little Madawaska Picnic Ground (KM 21.4); the pond between the Trailer Sanitation Station and Kearney Campground (KM 36); Eucalia Lake (KM 39); and the pond opposite the turn for Opeongo Road (KM 46.3). In addition, Opeongo Road north of the bridge where the pavement ends frequently offers views of moose feeding in spectacular settings.

Perhaps the best two trails for viewing moose in summer are Mizzy Lake (KM 15.4, especially along the old railway bed, which forms the northeastern section of the trail) and Beaver Pond (KM 45.2).

Although they might be encountered most places along the roadside, moose are usually viewed east of the old Park Museum (KM 20) than west of it. In addition to the sites discussed above some areas along the highway where frequent sightings have been made, particularly in early summer, include:

- Cache Lake region — KM 22.3 to KM 23.8.
- Track and Tower Trail region — KM 25.
- Hemlock Bluff Trail region — KM 27.2 to KM 27.6.
- Kearney Campground to Eucalia Lake — KM 36.5 to KM 39.
- Eos Lake to Beaver Pond Trail — KM 43.8 to KM 45.2.
- West Smith Lake to the Algonquin Logging Museum – KM 51.5 to KM 54.6.

Timber Wolf

Although one of the most difficult to see of all of Algonquin's large animals, at certain times of the year wolves are among the easiest to locate by their vocalizations. From late July through mid-October wolves are frequently heard from the Highway 60 vicinity. Wolves are social animals that travel in groups called packs. During midsummer, the pups are led from the dens to areas known as "rendezvous" sites, which are frequently beaver meadows (grassy areas where a beaver pond once existed) or bog edges. The pups are stationed at these sites and the adults bring them food from hunting excursions farther afield. Individual rendezvous sites may be used from several days up to several months at a time. While at these locations the pups are very vocal and readily respond to human howls.

Try listening or howling (refer to **When and How to See Wildlife** in Chapter 3)) from the following locations:

• Western Uplands Backpacking Trail — KM 3. Try from the bridge across the Oxtongue River at the start of the trail.
• Arowhon Road — 4.5 kilometres north from KM 15.4. Try at the intersection of this road and the old railway.
• KM 18. The bogs stretching to the south occasionally have wolves.
• Rock Lake Road — KM 40.3. Try at the intersection of the highway and Rock Lake Road; also try 2.8 kilometres south on Rock Lake Road.
• Sunday Creek — KM 42.6. The top of the rock cut just west of Sunday Creek and on the north side of the highway is an outstanding site. The eastern edge of the rock has a gradual slope easily climbed, but be careful.
• Eos Lake — KM 43.8. Wolves are regularly heard north of the lake.
• Beaver Pond Trail — KM 45.2. Wolves have been heard on either side of the highway from the trail entrance.
• Opeongo Road — KM 46.3. Try at the junction of the highway and Opeongo Road; also try up the Opeongo Road at the bridge where the pavement stops and the gravel begins.

- Brewer Lake — KM 48.6. I have only heard wolves here a couple of times, but the incredible echoes from across the lake make this an enjoyable spot to try.
- KM 54. Traditionally this has been a good spot. Wolves, when present, are usually heard north of the highway.

Although the above locations might offer a better chance of finding wolves, these animals have been heard at many other sites in the Corridor, including several highway campgrounds. However, I wouldn't recommend howling at these busy spots, particularly at 1:00 a.m!

Because you will be stopping along the highway, you must be safety conscious. Beware of soft shoulders on the roadside, but never stop on the pavement. If possible, pull off in parking lots of trails or picnic sites. Stand well off the highway when you are enjoying this magnificent music of the wilds.

Public Wolf Howls, excursions to hear wolves in the Corridor, are held on Thursdays in August if wolves have been located and weather permits. Since a Wolf Howl isn't attempted unless the naturalist staff has confirmed the presence of wolves the previous night, whether there will be a Howl is neither known nor disclosed until each Thursday morning. Thus, to determine if a Howl is being held on that day, either inquire at the Visitor Centre or any other Park office, or check the weekly bulletin *This Week in Algonquin* (the current issue is distributed each Thursday morning). If a Wolf Howl isn't held, an Evening Program will be offered instead.

Red Fox

People regularly encounter seemingly tame foxes in Algonquin. The tameness is invariably due to frequent contact with humans and not because of disease. Regardless, one should always be cautious and not touch or feed one of these animals. Although foxes are most active after sunset, they might be encountered in early morning or late evening. Probably the best way to find them is to drive the highway slowly after sunset and watch for their greenish eyes shining from the sides of the road.

One pair usually dens on the airfield at Mew Lake (KM 30.6). Thus, they are often seen in the Lake of Two Rivers and Mew Lake section of Highway 60. Another good area for seeing foxes is the highway near Rock Lake Road (KM 40.3).

Black Bear

Although relatively common throughout the Park, black bears are usually quite difficult to see primarily because of their shyness. Fortunate visitors might view a bear in early morning or late evening, the optimal times for encountering one, either crossing the road or foraging along open edges.

The best time of the year for seeing bears is mid-July to mid-August when raspberries, blueberries and cherries ripen. During this period, Opeongo and Rock Lake roads are worth driving slowly.

Very infrequently bears are encountered feeding on berry patches along trails. Generally they are long gone before you are even aware they were present. By walking trails as silently as possible (for if the bears hear you coming they quickly vanish), and either as early or as late in the day as possible, you might increase your slight chances of seeing a bear.

One area to check during the berry season is the old mill site at Whitefish Lake, which is accessed by driving south on Rock Lake Road until you reach the T junction where a left turn brings you to Rock Lake. Turn right at this intersection and park when you reach the bridge crossing the Madawaska River. *Do not obstruct the gate on the bridge.* You can walk across the bridge and follow the road to the large open area where a sawmill once stood. This location is popular with foraging bears.

Beaver

Algonquin is home to thousands of beaver colonies. Usually Beaver Pond Trail is an excellent spot to see beavers, particularly in late evening when they begin their daily activity. It is also an excellent place to learn about them, since their fascinating ecology is detailed in the trail guide.

Many of the small lakes and ponds along Highway 60 also support beavers. In fact, they can be observed right through the car window, a particularly enjoyable method during the biting fly season.

Don't be surprised if some of the beavers sport "earrings" — silver tags in their ears. Ear-tagged beavers are found throughout the Corridor and are part of university research programs. Some of the traditional spots to view beavers (in addition to the Beaver Pond Trail) in the Corridor are:

- Mew Lake — KM 30.1.
- Trailer Sanitation Station — KM 35.6. Check the pond approximately half a kilometre down the gravel road beyond the gate at the north end of the station turnaround.
- Eucalia Lake — KM 39. When visiting this excellent pond for beavers, one should park on the wider road shoulders below or above, not alongside, the guard posts bordering the pond.
- Ring-neck Pond — KM 41.2. Check the pond on the south side as well as the north side of the road.
- Opeongo Road — KM 46.3. The best areas to check are the sections of creek immediately above and below the bridge where the pavement ends and where Opeongo Lake meets Costello Creek. This latter spot can be viewed either from the boat launches to the south of the Opeongo Store or from the road just before it enters the store and boat launch access area.

Otter

Otters can be challenging to find yet are frequently seen along the Corridor. They are more easily encountered either in late summer and fall when family groups are eating together, or in early spring when individuals are feeding along the edge of the receding ice. Otters range widely and it is difficult to predict where they will be from day to day. However, in early spring (mid-April to mid-May) they may frequent good feeding areas for several days or longer. They are often seen along the edge of the ice when the lakes begin to open. At this time of year it is useful to check any waterway for dark debris on the edge of the ice. These dark piles may be droppings or remains of meals, indicating the presence of otters.

In any season Costello Creek along Opeongo Road (KM 46.3) is one of the best spots to see them. They might be encountered virtually anywhere open water is visible and are occasionally observed on the logs in Costello Lake across from the picnic ground. The best area to check, however, is Costello Creek between the south end of Opeongo Lake where the creek begins to the bridge where the pavement ends. Other areas where you might find otters are:

- Mizzy Lake Trail — KM 15.4. Mizzy is without question the best trail for encountering otters. They might be seen in any of the nine ponds visible from the trail. In particular, Mizzy Lake and Wolf Howl Pond offer excellent opportunities to view these amazing animals.
- Little Madawaska Picnic Grounds — KM 21.4. The pond on the north side of the highway occasionally has otters.
- Mew Lake — KM 30.1.
- Lake of Two Rivers Campground — KM 31.8. Otters are frequently present where the Madawaska River enters the lake.
- Ring-neck Pond — KM 41.2.

ALGONQUIN BIRDS

With its diverse array of habitats, particularly the mixture of northern coniferous and southern deciduous forests, Algonquin boasts an amazing mixture of species. Over half of the approximately 260 species recorded within the Park have been known to breed here. The majority of the nesting species can usually be encountered by searching the proper habitat, although frequently they are more easily heard than seen.

Two of the Park publications, *Birds of Algonquin Provincial Park* and the *Checklist and Seasonal Status of the Birds of Algonquin Provincial Park,* are invaluable in enjoying the birds found here. The first publication discusses birds by habitat and includes excellent colour photographs of 77 of the more common species. The latter summarizes all of the species recorded up to 1990 and provides useful bar graphs detailing their dates of occurrence.

Because of the popularity of Algonquin's birds, the interpretive program offers early morning interpretive Bird Walks and an Evening Program titled The Birds of Algonquin. Most of the interpretive trails traverse a number of habitats and thus offer a variety of birds. My favourite general trails for birdwatching are Whiskey Rapids and Beaver Pond trails. Spruce Bog Boardwalk and Mizzy Lake are two of the best trails for encountering northern species. Valuable tips on finding birds can be found in **OBSERVING WILDLIFE**.

Usually birders search for the northern "specialties" (birds whose ranges do not extend much farther south than Algonquin) during Park visits. With this in mind the better locations along the Corridor for some of these species will be provided. In addition, sites for encountering other popular species will be given.

Spruce Grouse

This tame northern grouse prefers the cool, dark recesses of northern bogs and boreal forest. For many birders Algonquin is the place of their first, and frequently only, sighting.

The males are at their ornate finest during the breeding season in April and early May. They strut around with their red eye combs inflamed and their tails noisily fanning. Males also perform "flutter flights" from the ground up to a nearby conifer and back down again. This noise often makes it easy to find a displaying bird. The males begin to show off again in early fall, but usually it is a more subdued performance. Tape recordings of female calls will attract the males, especially in spring. But before trying this read item number three in **Wildlife-viewing Etiquette** (in **OBSERVING WILDLIFE**).

Spruce Grouse are frequently observed in spruce and other conifers as they feed on the needles. Early morning and late afternoon are times of increased feeding activity in summer. From the middle of August to mid-September they feed on the needles of tamaracks. In late fall and winter the needles of spruces and pines are eaten. When searching for the birds, scan from ground level to about seven metres on the branches of coniferous trees. Listen for the snapping of needles while they are feeding. When flushed, Spruce Grouse exhibit a noisy, heavy flight that is usually very short in duration. An excellent article on finding this species was written by Ron Tozer and Ron Pittaway and appears in *Ontario Birds,* volume 8, number 2, a copy of which is available upon request at the Visitor Centre.

There are several excellent places where one can search for the sometimes elusive Spruce Grouse, and they are listed according to general ease in finding the birds. Of course, in any of these sites the birds might be either surprisingly easy or impossibly difficult to locate.

Spruce Bog Boardwalk — KM 42.5

This has traditionally been one of the best spots along the highway for Spruce Grouse. While you might encounter the birds along any part of the trail, there are at least two sections where more frequent observations have been made. Between Post 1 and the open bog mat before Post 2 there is an island of drier, more open ground. You will see a number of footpaths where grouse seekers have wandered, particularly on the left (north) side. Another good section lies between Posts 6 and 7, particularly in the vicinity of the trail register box.

Mizzy Lake Trail — KM 15.4

The best area for Spruce Grouse lies along the northern section of the trail in the Wolf Howl Pond vicinity, which can be reached by walking the trail (highly recommended for the diversity of birds that will be encountered), or by driving north on the Arowhon Road to the old railway bed junction and turning right. When you reach a locked gate, be sure to park to one side so that you don't block the road. Then proceed eastward on foot approximately one kilometre to Wolf Howl Pond.

Spruce Grouse are frequently seen either right of the rail bed picking up grit or feeding in the conifers fringing the edge of the rail bed. The section of rail bed just west of Wolf Howl Pond is good, but the 100 metres or so of rail bed southeast of Post 6 may produce the best results either along or in the vicinity of the rail bed.

Opeongo Road — KM 46.3

There are two excellent locations along this road for seeing Spruce Grouse. They are often seen picking up grit along the edge of the road, particularly at daybreak. However, foot searches just off the road may be required much of the time. The first place to look is the spruce woods bordering the left (west) side of the road 2.5 kilometres north from the highway. Grouse might be encountered from this point for about another half kilometre north, although from here to the orange gate on the road usually offers the best opportunities.

The second area worth checking is along the right (east) side of the road approximately half a kilometre north of the bridge where the pavement gives way to gravel. The birds usually reside in the strip of spruces between the road and the open bog mat to the east.

Mike's Bog — KM 54.2

To access this bog walk through the planted pines on the east side of the highway. An old road exists between the bog and the plantation. Travel down this road for about 200 metres and then walk down into the bog to your left.

Davies' Bog — KM 30

Another area to check if you still haven't succeeded is the coniferous forest surrounding Davies' Bog. This is usually a difficult spot to find them in, but they are here! The best way to access this site is to walk the Bat Lake Trail in reverse to Post 12. You might see Spruce Grouse on the trail, but odds are some searching will be required. Try scouring the spruces on either end of the boardwalk at Post 12.

Gray Jay

This northern bird is a delight to encounter, not only because of its gentle nature but also because it will readily take food from your hand. At times it seems hard to believe that a bird so seemingly meek could survive the severe Algonquin winters. Yet Gray Jays do so quite nicely, principally because they continually store food throughout the other seasons. It is fascinating to watch the birds in action. After accepting a morsel of bread, cookie, raisin or whatever your offering might be, the bird rolls each piece in its mouth, coating it with saliva. Then it flies off, stashing the package in a tree, frequently under a piece of lichen or loose bark. The saliva cements the package securely in the hiding place, which quite often is robbed by Blue Jays, experts in shadowing their cousins.

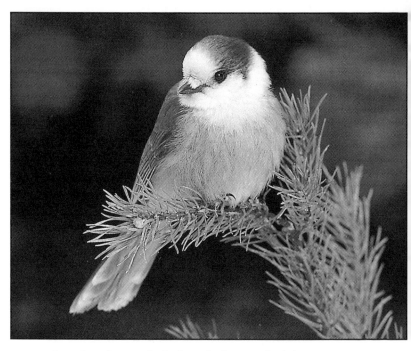

Gray Jays frequently find you before you find them.

This sticky coating may also serve to keep the food fresh, for it may be many months before the stash is eaten.

When Gray Jays approach you for handouts, you will often find that their legs are decorated with colourful bands that jingle-jangle when they fly. Dan Strickland, longtime chief park naturalist, has been studying these birds for almost 20 years. By banding the young each year he has been able to document how long they live, as well as where they range and who they mate with.

This amazing study is one of the longest of its kind and is truly a labour of love for Dan. You can help by recording the dates and locations of your sightings of banded jays, plus the band colour combinations on each of their legs. For example, red over standard (a standard aluminum band that is always present on one of the legs) on the bird's left leg and yellow over dark green on the right leg. Your valuable observations can be dropped off at the Visitor Centre or at the gates, if that is more convenient.

Since Gray Jays frequent much the same habitat as Spruce Grouse, it comes as no surprise that you might well encounter both species in the same area. Thus, any of the aforementioned areas for seeing grouse might produce jays. Unfortunately there are times, particularly in late spring and early summer, when Gray Jays become secretive and tough to find, even in the best of locations. They become easier to find as summer progresses and are virtually guaranteed to be seen in fall and winter. Refer to **OBSERVING WILDLIFE** for tips detailing how you might attract them (although these birds tend to find you first!) and be sure to carry some spare food with you. Some regular "hot spots" to try are:

Opeongo Road — KM 46.3

Several pairs have territories along this road. While they might be encountered almost anywhere here, try at the Costello Picnic Grounds, at the junction of the logging road 2.5 kilometres north of the highway, and just past the bridge where the pavement ends.

Mizzy Lake Trail — KM 15.4

The old railway at the northeastern section of the trail is the best area for them. They can usually be found between West Rose Lake and the gate near the junction of the rail bed and Arowhon Road.

Spruce Bog Boardwalk — KM 42.5

The birds might find you virtually anywhere on this trail.

Mew Lake Campground — KM 30.6

Try walking around the northeast part of the campground, particularly in fall and winter.

Black-backed Woodpecker

Another "northerner" frequently sought by birders, Black-backed Woodpeckers also frequent the bog and coniferous habitats of the former two species. They are most easily encountered by listening for their slow, heavy pecking and their sharp calls, which sound like a noisy kiss to the back of your fingers. The best way, though, is to imitate or play back the call of a Barred Owl. Not only does this call draw in Black-backs, it is also guaranteed to attract any other woodpecker within hearing range. But before using playbacks read **Wildlife-viewing Etiquette** in **OBSERVING WILDLIFE**.

An aid to finding these birds involves the distinctive signs they leave behind when feeding. One of their favourite foods is the larvae of bark beetles, which tunnel, as their name suggests, under the bark of trees. Black-backed Woodpeckers particularly relish the species that inhabit spruces. To get at the beetles these woodpeckers strip the bark from large sections of infected trees. Thus, if you find spruces with large sections of the trunk recently stripped clean (the barkless trunk appearing orange), the woodpecker is probably not far away. These birds are year-round residents, and in summer they frequently nest near beaver ponds.

Sites where you might encounter these birds include all of the places described for Spruce Grouse, especially the northeastern section of the Mizzy Lake Trail and along Opeongo Road. I would also recommend you search at these other locations:

Western Uplands Backpacking Trail — KM 3

The section of the trail just past the bridge at the trail start is an excellent place for these birds.

Oxtongue Logging Road Pond — KM 8

This road, closed to private vehicles, leads north from the highway. Park either on the highway shoulder or to the side of the gate, leaving the access unob-structed. Walk approximately one kilometre along the road until you arrive at a large pond on the left. Black-backed Woodpeckers are often encountered near the pond.

Boreal Chickadee

This northern counterpart of the Black-capped Chickadee becomes extremely silent and thus next to impossible to find during the nesting season. However, as summer progresses they become increasingly vocal, and by mid-August they can be found in most of the locations where Spruce Grouse and Black-backed Woodpeckers frequent.

In addition to the two locations listed for Black-backed Woodpeckers, both excellent for Boreal Chickadees in late summer, also try the following sites:

• The old railway bed on the north side of the highway — KM 22.3.
• The south edge of the Mew Lake Airfield — KM 30.6.
• The trail around the Algonquin Logging Museum — KM 54.6

OTHER SPECIES

A few more of the commonly sought-after species will be profiled here. Additional information concerning any of the Park birds can be obtained from the naturalists at the Visitor Centre.

Barred Owl

The booming calls and eerie cackles of Barred Owls, Algonquin's most common owl, are regularly heard at night. They usually respond to playbacks of taped calls, such as those found on the inexpensive cassette *Voices of Algonquin,* and even answer to human imitations. Before using playbacks refer to **Wildlife-viewing Etiquette** in **OBSERVING WILDLIFE**. Barred Owls are also easily "squeaked in" (refer to **When and How to See Wildlife** in the same chapter), particularly just before sunset.

You may wish to participate in an interpretive Night Walk if one is offered during your stay. Barred Owls are often encountered on these outings.

While you might hear these birds virtually anywhere in the Highway Corridor, some of the more regular locations are provided.

Western Uplands Backpacking Trail — KM 3

Try from the bridge at the beginning of the trail.

Whiskey Rapids Trail — KM 7.2

I have frequently heard Barred Owls from the highway near the trail entrance.

Hardwood Hill Picnic Ground — KM 16.7

Either right from the picnic site or along the logging road leading north directly across the highway is a traditional location from which to hear these birds.

Source Lake Road — KM 20.1

Approximately 0.4 kilometre north of the highway is a good place to try.

Hemlock Bluff Trail — KM 27.2

Barred Owls have been heard from both sides of the highway at this location.

Trailer Sanitation Station — KM 35.6

Try near the pond approximately half a kilometre north from the Sanitation Station turnaround.

Rock Lake Road — KM 40.3

Try at the intersection of this road and the highway. Also try one kilometre up the road on the north side of the highway at this intersection. Here you will encounter a gate marking the end to public travel on this road.

Spruce Bog Boardwalk — KM 42.5

I always enjoy listening from the top of the rock cut that lies between the parking lot and the bridge crossing the creek. The eastern edge of the rocks has a gradual slope, but take care in climbing up.

Brewer Lake — KM 48.6

The parking lot offers safe parking as well as an excellent listening location.

Leaf Lake Ski Trail — KM 53.9

I have heard Barred Owls in the vicinity of the trail entrance.

Pileated Woodpecker

This spectacular crow-sized woodpecker is common throughout Algonquin and is frequently encountered along Highway 60. Their easily recognized excavations, made in search of carpenter ants, can be seen in a number of dead trees along the highway edge. Usually they produce large, often gigantic rectangular or oval holes quite visible from a great distance. Listen for their distinctive *kuk-kuk-kuk*. An imitation of these or Barred Owl calls may attract the birds.

Pileated Woodpeckers frequently fly across the highway in late afternoon. Their stiff flight with massive wings flashing bold black-and-white patterns is quite distinctive.

These birds are common and can be found along any trail, particularly, but not exclusively, on trails through mature hardwood forests. Some locations where Pileated Woodpeckers are often seen include:

- Hardwood Lookout Trail — KM 13.8.
- Found Lake — KM 20. Right behind the old Park Museum is a fine spot to search. A trail that encircles Found Lake starts directly behind the buildings.
- Highway 60 between KM 25.5 and KM 26.3.
- Highway 60 between KM 28.5 and KM 28.8.

- Rock Lake Road — south from KM 40.3.
- Booth's Rock Trail — nine kilometres south from KM 40.3.

Common Loon

This is a relatively easy bird to encounter because virtually all of the larger lakes support at least one pair. Even the busiest lakes usually have loons that produce young each year. It is an enjoyable sight to see a family group in action, with both parents feeding small fish to the one or two young, and also occasionally giving them rides on their backs. The vocalizations of this bird are an important part of many Algonquin experiences because its spine-tingling calls are among the wildest sounds in the world. Rare is the campsite near water that lacks their mournful wails and haunting laughter at night. The cassette *Voices of Algonquin* not only has outstanding recordings of these birds but also offers explanations as to what the different calls mean.

Because loons nest at the edge of the water, their nests are frequently discovered by canoeists. If you are in a canoe and locate a nest, don't spend any more than a brief moment admiring the birds before you leave them in privacy. Repeated harassment, regardless of how unintentional it might be, may result in a loss of the eggs.

Loons are often seen in larger lakes right along the highway. Although generally distinctive birds, they might be confused with Common Mergansers, a fish-eating duck. Loons are larger with heavier heads and necks. In summer they display a bold checkered back pattern. The mergansers are smaller and females, which are the only adults present in summer, have reddish-brown heads that contrast with a gray back. Usually they have many more than two young in tow; in fact, the average brood size is 12. Viewing sites for loons include:

- Smoke Lake — KM 15.2.
- Lake of Two Rivers — KM 32.3 to KM 33; KM 33.8; KM 34.5.
- Costello Lake — KM 46.3.
- Brewer Lake — KM 48.6.

SCENIC VIEWS

The Highway Corridor is rich in striking scenery and breathtaking vantage points. Each season dresses the roadside scenery in new and dramatic apparel. Lakes come alive under the swirling mists of late summer, and in autumn the maple hills transform into an extravaganza of colour. **SEASONAL HIGHLIGHTS** details the best time for viewing fall colours.

Of course, beauty is in the eye of the beholder, and undoubtedly you will find a number of other sites along the highway that appeal to you. The following is simply a guide to some of the more dramatic locations for viewing and/or photography in the Highway Corridor.

Tea Lake — KM 9.2

The only drawback to this site are the telephone lines situated along the lake side of the highway.

Smoke Creek — KM 12

This creek offers excellent fall colours along its edge and also reflections of these in its water, particularly early in the morning. The old parking lot on the east side of the bridge is the best spot for enjoying the view.

Smoke Lake — KM 13.5

A good view of maple hills and Smoke Lake is offered at this point from the highway.

Hardwood Lookout Trail — KM 13.8

As its name suggests, this trail has a lookout over hardwood hills. The views from the other trails offering lookouts are generally more dynamic.

Late summer morning mists add another element to the beauty of Smoke Lake and other Park waterways.

Smoke Lake — KM 14.8

The pull-off on the lake side is an ideal place to park. At daybreak in August the point jutting into Smoke Lake has the sun rising behind it. The mists that rise off the lake at this time of year create a backdrop that is simply outstanding.

Hardwood Hill — KM 16.6

You might wish to park at the picnic ground just 0.1 kilometre past this point. The view to the west is particularly striking during the peak of the fall colours.

Track and Tower Trail — KM 25

A superb view of Cache Lake is offered at Post 7.

Two Rivers Hill — KM 28.5

This view to the east is particularly attractive at daybreak. Mists frequently shroud the far hills, and the pine at the lower left of the hill projects nicely against this backdrop. A beautiful hardwood forest covers the hillside along the north side of the road and is quite attractive in the autumn.

Two Rivers Trail — KM 31

A fine lookout is afforded from Post 7.

Lake of Two Rivers — KM 32.5

Various points along the road offer excellent views of the lake. The far side of the lake is alive with colour in the fall. This spot is also spectacular at daybreak, particularly when cloaked with mists in late summer.

Centennial Ridges Trail — two kilometres south from KM 37.6

Some of the finest vantage points in the Corridor are situated along this rugged trail.

Lookout Trail — KM 39.7

An excellent view of the rolling hills typical of this side of the Park is available from the highway. Even after the maples have faded this site still offers colourful views when the hills blaze with golden poplars.

One of the most dramatic views of the western uplands is achieved from the top of this walking trail. An unmarked trail leading to a fine view is located directly across the highway from the west end of the parking lot. Remember that all lookouts lack railings, so make sure you keep children under control at all times.

Booth's Rock Trail — nine kilometres south of KM 40.3

The view over Rock Lake from Post 7 is simply spectacular.

Algonquin Visitor Centre — KM 45

The viewing deck at the Visitor Centre offers a breathtaking view, equally marvellous at any time of the year.

Costello Creek — four kilometres north from KM 46.3

This boggy creek with a dramatic cliff rising behind is a beautiful area year-round. Several spots along the road offer enjoyable views, especially in late summer and fall. My favourite place is just beyond the bridge where the pavement ends.

Brewer Lake — KM 48.6

The hillside across the lake contains some of the best fall colour along the highway. If you climb to the top of the rock cut on the north side of the highway, an even better view is offered.

POINTS OF HISTORICAL INTEREST

Algonquin has had a long and fascinating history. Evidence of activities in earlier times can often be located right along the Highway Corridor. The following is a brief guide to some of the more interesting historic sites located in the Corridor. Other sites in the highway vicinity but accessible only by canoe will be discussed under **Canoeing in the Corridor**.

The Ottawa, Arnprior and Parry Sound (OA & PS) Railway

The rail bed of this historic railway, reputed to have been one of the busiest in Canada with a train every 20 minutes, can be viewed at several locations. In fact, sections of the rail bed are utilized by three of the interpretive and both backpacking trails.

J. R. Booth, a lumber baron prominent in the Park's history, built this railway between 1894 and 1896. Initially it was used for hauling logs and grain, but soon it became important in transporting visitors to Algonquin. It remained the only way to reach the Park until the arrival of the highway in the mid-1930s.

The easy access provided by Highway 60 became the nemesis of the OA & PS. The section of railway between

The OA & PS Railway was extremely busy in its heyday, with trains reportedly as frequent as every 20 mintues.

Lake of Two Rivers and Cache Lake was discontinued in 1933. Service from the east to Lake of Two Rivers was terminated in 1946, and from the west to Cache Lake in 1959.

For simplicity, access to the old railway bed will be given starting from the west end of the Park.

Mizzy Lake Trail — KM 15.4

The northeast section of the trail lies on the rail bed. This can also be reached by driving up Arowhon Road approximately four kilometres to a crossroads. The road crossing Arowhon Road is actually the rail bed of the OA & PS Railway.

Source Lake Road — KM 20.1

Drive north until you hit the dip at the Madawaska River (here just a small creek) crossing. The railway abutments are clearly visible on either side of the road.

Highway 60 Crossing — KM 22.3

You will see a small parking area on the north side of the road. The parking lot on the south side of the road is used by the staff of Camp Tanamakoon, a girls' camp. Although the railway actually crosses the highway, only the section on the north side is walkable. Look for a footpath leading northwest. As you face the woods, it will be to your left. After travelling through an alder thicket, you will enter an open area where the rail bed becomes apparent. If you continue, you will eventually reach Source Lake Road.

Cache Lake — KM 23.5

Drive into the Cache Lake parking lot. When you near the boat launch the rail bed can be easily viewed to your left behind the shelter. The section to your right is a little more difficult to see because a planation of pines obscures the rail bed. However, a footpath traverses the pines. This path is well worth exploring since it travels along the railway platform in front of the remnants of the Highland Inn, a grand railway hotel. The hotel was built in 1908 and expanded in 1910. This elegant building was demolished in 1957, two years before the rail service was discontinued from the west. All that remains are a few walls bordering the railway platform, moss-covered stairs leading up to the site of the inn and an old fire hydrant. If you travel east along the rail bed, you will arrive at the remains of a trestle that spanned a bay of Cache Lake.

Track and Tower Trail — KM 25

The railway bed forms part of this trail and the history of the railway is discussed in the trail guide booklet. The remains of several trestles can also be viewed from this excellent trail.

It is intriguing to think that during the First World War armed guards stood sentinel on these trestles to thwart potential saboteurs. Use of this section of the railway was discontinued in 1933.

Highland Backpacking Trail — KM 29.7

One can access the old railway bed by walking 2.8 kilometres on this trail. At this point the rail bed intersects the Highland Trail, and the section leading northeast forms part of the trail.

Airfield — KM 30.6

Drive past the campground office until you reach the T junction at the old airfield. The parking lot is to your left. You can access the old railway by walking southeast across the airfield. Along the far side you will encounter a dirt road running east to west. A side branch to the south takes you to a footpath leading to a bridge across the Madawaska River. The rail bed lies on the far side of the river. You can also travel west on the dirt road until you reach a side trail of the Track and Tower Trail. Travel along it until you reach Post 15. Here the trail follows the old rail bed.

Rock Lake — 7.5 kilometres south from KM 40.3

When you arrive at the T junction where you turn left to reach the Rock Lake Campground and Booth's Rock Trail, you have reached the old railway bed. The rail bed is used as a road from this point to the parking lot for the Booth's Rock Trail. The last section of the Booth's Rock Trail also lies on this rail bed.

Other Historical Sites

A few additional points of interest are detailed here.

Tote Road and Building Remains — KM 7.2

These sites are located along the Whiskey Rapids Trail. The 45 kilometres of tote road extended from Dorset (west of Algonquin) to the north end of Canoe Lake and crossed the Oxtongue River at the Tea Lake Dam. Horse-drawn wagons in summer and sleighs in winter were used to haul supplies in the late 1800s. The tote road forms the portion of the trail between Post 10 and the parking lot. Between Posts 9 and 10 the rotting remains of either a halfway house or shelters used by river drivers are visible.

Tea Lake Dam — KM 8.1

The dam is located on the Oxtongue River at the end of the Tea Lake Dam Picnic Grounds. This modern dam, built in 1964, replaces a much earlier wooden version that Tom Thomson, one of Canada's most renowned artists, painted in 1915. It is believed that Thomson's first trip to Algonquin involved a camping trip to this very spot.

James Dickson Memorial — KM 20

Along the stairs to the old Park Museum you will find this memorial. Dickson was the provincial land surveyor who, through his recommendations and surveys, was instrumental in the formation of Algonquin Park. At the top of the stairs lies the former Park Museum, opened in 1953 and last used in 1992.

Frank A. MacDougall Memorial — KM 23.3

MacDougall was the park superintendent from 1931 to 1941 and was responsible for introducing the airplane as a tool in fire detection. The MacDougall Parkway, the section of Highway 60 between the Park boundaries, was named in his honour in 1976. The memorial is located in the pull-off area on the north side of the highway.

Highland Inn — KM 23.5

This site is described in the Cache Lake entry in the **OA & PS Railway** section.

Airfield — KM 30.6

The airfield, situated between Mew Lake and Lake of Two Rivers, can be reached by driving past the campground office for Mew Lake. A parking lot is located to the left of the T junction.

This extensive open area was cleared in 1935 as an emergency landing strip for aircraft. Although never used for this purpose, planes have occasionally landed when short on fuel. It has also been used for a variety of activities, including fire control demonstrations and fly-in breakfasts.

McRae Mill Site — KM 30.6

Only a few subtle remains identify the site of this former sawmill built in 1931 and last used in 1942. It lies along the old railway bed on the far side of the Madawaska River on the south edge of the airfield. To reach the site travel across the airfield to the southeast side where you will find a dirt road. Take the short side branch that leads toward the Madawaska River and follow a foot-path to a bridge across the river. Cross the bridge and turn left on the old railway bed. You will eventually reach an opening where the mill formerly stood.

Alexander Kirkwood Memorial — KM 31.8

Algonquin Park owes its existence to the incredible foresight of Alexander Kirkwood. In 1885 Kirkwood, a clerk in the office of the Ontario Department of Crown Lands, proposed the idea of a park to conserve the forests and protect the headwaters of rivers flowing from it. A plaque on the large rock on the north side of the road honours this man.

Hammer and Sickle — KM 35.3

These figures with the year 34 can be discerned on the rock cut just to the east of the lane on the south side of the highway. It is wise to park past this point, possibly near the entrance to East Beach (KM 35.4), because cars unexpectedly speed over the hill from the Lake of Two Rivers direction. Since Highway 60 was built in the mid-1930s, it is presumed that these figures were chiselled in the rock by a Russian road worker.

McRae Mill Site — eight kilometres south from KM 40.3

This sawmill was last used in 1979. The site can be accessed by travelling south on the Rock Lake Road to the T junction near the campground. Turn right at this junction and drive to the gate on the bridge. Park without blocking the bridge and walk across it. The mill lies only a few hundred metres past the bridge.

Barclay Estate — nine kilometres south from KM 40.3

This site lies on the Booth's Rock Trail. You can take a shortcut to it by travelling backward on the trail along the old rail bed of the OA & PS Railway. When you turn right at Post 9, you will have reached the grounds of the estate.

The estate was built at the turn of the century by Judge Gregor Barclay, who was a relative of J. R. Booth, the lumber baron who built the railway. The estate was last used in 1953, and all that remains now are foundations, tennis courts and the remnants of the docks.

Harkness Memorial — six kilometres north from KM 46.3

Dr. William John Knox Harkness, the man responsible for the establishment of the Harkness Laboratory of Fisheries Research, which is located at this site, is honoured here. The plaque is located on a cairn only a few hundred metres past the parking lot on the north side of the store. Just walk along the road (closed to unauthorized vehicles) that hugs the shoreline past the parking lot. The cairn is situated on the point to the right of the first building you come to.

Dr. Harkness was a professor of limnology at the University of Toronto and was also chief of the Fish and Wildlife Branch of the Ontario Department of Lands and Forests.

St. Anthony Lumber Company Railway Spur Line — KM 52

Take the dirt road running east just south of West Smith Lake. Watch carefully for a trail on the north (left) side of the road, halfway between the highway and the end of this short road. The trail lies on the railway spur line that once ran from Whitney to Opeongo Lake. The line extended north from here to Little McCauley Lake and then south back to the highway at the north end of Brewer Lake. Short sections of both Highway 60 and Opeongo Road are now located along parts of the rail bed on which timber was once transported. The spur line was built in 1902 and was abandoned in 1926.

The site of a former sawmill is located along this spur line between West Smith and Whitney Lakes. However, access may be difficult, since parts of this rail bed may not be passable due to erosion and dense tree growth.

Algonquin Logging Museum — KM 54.6

This museum exhibits a spectacular assortment of historical logging buildings, structures and equipment chronologically arranged along a scenic trail. While some of the buildings, such as the camboose (a log structure with bunks arranged around a large central fireplace), are accurate replicas, others, including two ranger cabins, are the original buildings transported from their former sites.

Other highlights include a steam locomotive and replicated log chute and dam. The *William M.*, a steam-warping tug also known as an alligator, towed log booms across large lakes and is one of only three still in existence. This amazing steam-driven boat could travel both across water by use of paddle wheels and over land by winch and log skids. The entrance road crosses the St. Anthony Lumber Company Spur Line described in the entry of that title.

Canoeing in the Corridor

My favourite way of exploring the Highway Corridor is by canoe. The pleasure of silently paddling along a winding river or creek and rounding a bend only to encounter a moose or heron is truly a wilderness experience. Regardless of how busy the season might be, if you paddle at daybreak your canoe will frequently be the only one out there. In addition to seeing more wildlife you get the added bonus of experiencing the most beautiful time of day.

Canoeing in the Corridor will also enable you to visit a number of historical sites as well as participate in special interpretive events. Be aware that each person in a canoe is required to have a regulation life jacket, now known by the fancy term Personal Flotation Device (PFD). In addition, some sort of bailing equipment and a PSD (Personal Signalling Device — i.e., a whistle) are required. A must for any canoe trip is the *Canoe Routes of Algonquin Provincial Park* map brochure, which is not only an essential navigational tool but also a wonderful keepsake of the trip.

Available Services

Canoes can be rented at the Portage Store (KM 14.1), the Opeongo Store (north from KM 46.3) and Bartlett Lodge (on Cache Lake south from KM 23.5). The first two rental places also offer canoe pickup and delivery, as well as complete outfitting services.

Free canoe demonstrations and lessons are usually offered in summer at various campground beaches. Check *This Week in Algonquin* and the bulletin boards to see if these are being offered during your visit.

The Portage Store in some years offers guided day outings for which the fee includes all equipment and a lunch. The interpretive program offers free guided outings where participants bring their own equipment (frequently rented from one of the stores) and a lunch.

These casual outings offer some canoeing instruction but focus on the Park's natural and human history encountered on the outing.

Canoe Centres on Canoe and Opeongo lakes sell permits and provide free information and advice for Interior canoeing and camping. The *Canoe Routes of Algonquin Provincial Park* map brochures are available here as well as at the gates and museums.

Recommended Short Trips

The Highway Corridor is a doorway into the Park Interior. Here there are a number of different access points from which to start overnight trips. In this section only excursions of a day or less will be discussed. For a description of highlights requiring longer trips refer to **The Park Interior** in Chapter 8.

The following trips are all quite short, often a half day at most, but several have the option of being extended into a full day (or even longer) excursion if desired. It is always a good idea to pack some food and beverages even for a half-day trip. Remember that cans and bottles are prohibited from the Park Interior and that Interior camping permits must be obtained if you decide to stay overnight.

The Oxtongue River — (KM 3)

This is a beautiful river to canoe because it gently twists and bends through its length. The spruces and firs that line its shores frequently harbour northern birds such as Boreal Chickadees and Black-backed Woodpeckers. The "quick-three-beer" whistles of Olive-sided Flycatchers follow you around each bend, and the incessant chatter of red squirrels continually scolds your intrusion. Great Blue Herons frequently flush ahead, while Common Mergansers spatter across the river's surface.

There are many options for accessing this river, including starting at the Portage Store on Canoe Lake and paddling down through Bonita into Tea Lake. Once on the river, only a couple of short portages (trails identified by black-and-yellow signs depicting a canoe being carried, used for bypassing rapids) are encountered between the Western Uplands Backpacking Trail and the starting point.

Another option, one which I frequently use, is to launch at the Western Uplands Backpacking Trail and paddle west to the first portage at Lower Twin Falls. About halfway down this route there is one short stretch of shallow water (shown as rapids on the *Canoe Routes of Algonquin Provincial Park* map brochure) where you may wish to walk your canoe through. To be sure, it is always best to wear running shoes when canoeing! You can also carry your canoe around the south side. When the water is high, you can float over the rocks, but my experience is that this usually isn't the case.

Watch for the beautiful trumpet-shaped nets of caddisflies, which lie on the upstream side of these gentle rapids. The current enters the net's large opening and passes through to the narrow end where the insect larva waits for the minute particles of food to arrive.

The portage around Lower Twin Falls is an excellent place to end this part of the trip. The rocks along the pretty little falls, actually more of a rapids, offer excellent sites on which to have lunch.

If you feel like continuing down the river, another short portage lies less than a half kilometre ahead. This is a tricky one, since the banks are steep and the current strong. If you are planning to continue, beware of this awkward portage and be prepared in advance to hug the south (left) shoreline as you approach the rapids.

If you are travelling with another couple and have the luxury of a second vehicle, you may wish to leave one just past the Park boundary where a short portage will bring you to the highway from the river. This allows you to paddle downstream the entire trip. Be aware of the extra distance involved and that the second portage west of the Western Uplands Backpacking Trail is only about halfway to the Park boundary.

The Madawaska River — (KM 35.4)

This trip is one of my favourite routes, not just because of this delightful winding river but also due to the plentiful wildlife I have encountered along its length. The route also holds a special place in my heart since I spend time at its source (Source Lake) in the summer and live at its mouth (Arnprior, where it joins the Ottawa River) in the winter. I generally put in my canoe at the boat launch at the Lake of Two Rivers East Beach (KM 35.4). From here I journey down to Whitefish Lake and back. Of course, one can make this a longer trip if desired, for it is an easy journey to Rock Lake from Whitefish. If you are camping at Pog Lake Campground, you can start paddling from the lake, since the Madawaska flows through it. There is only one very short portage around Pog Lake Dam.

I have often met moose, otter, Great Blue Herons, Common Mergansers, muskrats and Black Ducks on this river. There are some excellent stretches that are bordered by northern woods where Boreal Chickadees and Gray Jays might be found. Another attraction is the historic OA & PS Railway, which follows the river for much of this route. Watch for the old culverts, in particular the one constructed of stones, which you pass by on the right (west) side of the river between Lake of Two Rivers and Pog Lake Dam. The more modern circular one contains a beaver dam.

Also watch in the water for the incredible green growth of freshwater sponge that covers submerged rocks and logs, particularly just below the dam. Sometimes it looks like fingerlike extensions; other times it appears as circular patches on the rocks. Be sure to pick up a piece (carefully so as not to upset the canoe) to feel its peculiar texture and sniff the curious aroma. If you are paddling along this route in late summer, keep your eyes peeled for the bizarre white blooms of turtlehead, an uncommon flower in Algonquin that peeks from the shores below the dam.

At the point where the Madawaska River meets the bay at the north end of Whitefish Lake (where the group campground is situated) you will come across a shallow area on the left side of the creek. When you get there, look carefully for snapping turtles that lie submerged with only their snouts projecting out of the water.

Once you reach Whitefish Lake, the large sand beach at the group campground is a perfect spot to have lunch and a swim. Alternately you can paddle over to the rocky points directly across the bay or along the east shore. From there you can either continue down Whitefish Lake or return. The top end of Whitefish Lake is really a river, but it eventually widens before reaching Rock Lake. If you are travelling with another couple, you might consider leaving a vehicle at Rock Lake and make this a one-way trip. Be aware, however, that motorboats are permitted on Whitefish and Rock lakes.

Costello Creek — north from KM 46.3

Even though this trip is shorter than the two previously discussed routes and follows a public road for a short part of its length, Costello Creek remains one of my favourite Algonquin waterways. Not only have I encountered numerous animals on this creek, but the scenery is frequently so stunning that I just stop paddling and become absorbed in the surrounding beauty. Several of the photographs in *Algonquin Seasons* were taken along this creek.

The best access is from the boat launch by the Opeongo Store. Just past the store there are parking lots where you can leave your vehicle. Motorboats are allowed on Opeongo Lake but cannot travel on Costello Creek. A sign indicating that motorboats are prohibited is situated on the tiny island just south of the boat launch.

Try starting your trip at the crack of dawn. At this time there is usually little wind, and wildlife is far more active, unlike humans. Canoe south from the docks into the narrowing of Opeongo that becomes Costello Creek. On the left side is an open floating bog where the carnivorous bog plants sundew and pitcher plant can easily be found. A number of beaver lodges, some active, are also located along the edge of this bog mat.

When you enter the narrow channel before the creek opens up again, beware of a couple of large submerged rocks that might scrape the bottom of your canoe. There is a deep channel here, so only a little bit of care is required to avoid these infrequent objects.

After the narrows, the creek winds through a fairly extensive bog mat punctuated with cattail clumps near this end. Great Blue Herons frequently fly just ahead of your canoe and land a couple of bends farther along, only to be flushed when you again draw near. Sometimes you will paddle around a bend and meet up with an American Bittern. Although they will fly to escape, occasionally they point their beaks into the air and freeze, relying on their breast stripes to blend in with the vegetation and render them invisible. Their strange song, resembling a stake being driven into soft mud, is often heard along the creek. Dead trees resulting from raised water levels in the lake provide homes and perches for a variety of birds. Tree Swallows twitter and Eastern Kingbirds angrily buzz over your canoe as you approach them. The "quick-three-beer" whistles of Olive-sided Flycatchers taunt you from the tops of these snags, while the sleepy "sweet-sweet-Canada-Canada-Canada" of White-throated Sparrows drift from the spruces.

As soon as you pass through the narrows, the overwhelming beauty of this route becomes apparent. The open expanse of bog mat is bordered by a neat fringe of black spruce and tamarack. These trees start out large near the high ground but shrink in size as they approach the open creek. Farther along, a rugged cliff towers to the east of the creek. This dramatic scenery is transformed into a wonderland in August when glowing mists swirl into the warming rays of the rising sun.

Moose feed in the creek in early summer, and I have also observed deer frequenting its edges. Otters inhabit the creek and mink hunt along it. Watch for droppings of these animals in the crevice of the huge boulder that you eventually paddle around. Just past this boulder is a small "island" on the right that is a wonderful spot for a rest or a lunch break. Just beyond that lies Opeongo Road. If you wish to continue along the creek, you can carry the canoe over the road or, if the water is high, you can paddle under it through the culvert.

If you walk along the paved road on the south side of the bridge, on your left you will encounter a footpath leading up the hillside. There are large scattered rocks along the hill that will offer you a view over part of the creek you have just canoed. They also make good seats for lunch.

Other Day Trips

While the aforementioned are my favourite three routes, a number of other trips are available. These, however, include lakes on which motorboats are allowed (none of the above routes have motorboat activity, apart from the very end of the Madawaska route in Whitefish Lake and the start of the Costello Creek route at Opeongo Lake). Also, with their larger expanses of water these lakes can be a challenge to paddle on a windy day. However, a number of fascinating historical sites are situated along some of these routes, so if the day is calm, you may wish to try them.

Canoe Lake — KM 14.1

Canoe Lake is one of the busiest lakes in the Park, largely because it is the major launching point for canoe trips into the Interior. Motorboats also ply its waters, taking leaseholders to their cottages or carrying people and supplies to the children's camps (Wapomeo and Ahmek) situated on the lake. I would recommend canoeing on this lake as early as possible in the morning when motorboat activity might be low. However, you will undoubtedly meet a few on the return trip.

The north end of the lake is where everything of interest is located. On the north-central point lies a cairn well worth visiting. A small dock offers a place to access the short footpaths leading to the cairn. A rather obtrusive totem pole erected beside the cairn by a neighbouring camp is an obvious sign that you are at the right spot. The cairn was erected in September 1917 in honour of the famous Canadian artist Tom Thomson, who drowned in Canoe Lake on July 8, 1917. Friends of Thomson, including artists who later became known as the Group of Seven, erected this monument. The wording on the bronze plate was composed by J. E. H. MacDonald. The epitaph on the plaque is so moving that I feel compelled to reprint it here in case you don't get the opportunity to visit the cairn:

> *To the memory of Tom Thomson, artist, woodsman and guide, who was drowned in Canoe Lake, July 8, 1917. He lived humbly but passionately with the wild. It made him brother to all untamed things of nature. It drew him apart and revealed itself to him wonderfully. It sent him out from the woods only to show these revelations through his art, and it took him to itself at last.*

As the inscription states, Thomson drowned in this very lake. His death is shrouded in controversy that has fuelled much conjecture and even a book and movie. Whether he drowned accidentally or was killed is of no consequence to this publication. Let it be enough that the magnificence of Algonquin captured his heart and that this beauty lives on through his art.

On the far shore directly west of the cairn lies the former townsite of Mowat. Established by the Gilmour Lumber Company in 1893, Mowat was also the site of the first Park headquarters. By 1896 at least 600 men lived here. However, the thriving lumber town soon became quiet when the mill closed down in 1900, following the bankruptcy of the Gilmour Company. Apparently the bankruptcy was at least in part due to a failed and incredibly costly scheme to transport logs from Mowat to Trenton. The logs were floated down Canoe Lake and the Oxtongue River to Lake of Bays. An alligator dragged the booms to Baysville where an endless chain-and-trough system dragged the logs overland to Raven Lake. From here logs were eventually floated down the Trent River system. Unfortunately the journey took so long that by the time the logs arrived at their destination they were in such poor shape that they were practically unusable.

Mowat soon became popular with tourists. A lodge was opened in 1913 and became the summer headquarters for Tom Thomson. The busy atmosphere at Mowat was short-lived, however. Mowat Lodge burnt down in 1920, was rebuilt at a new location, then burnt down again in 1930. The once-thriving town of Mowat finally deteriorated into a virtual ghost town.

North from the Mowat townsite the rail bed of the OA & PS Railway is accessible by taking either of the two branches of the lake. The left branch travels up picturesque Potter Creek to the railway bridge. The right branch will eventually bring you to the old rail bed along bottom of Joe Lake, but first you have to make a short portage around Joe Lake Dam. Two major buildings were situated in this area. Joe Lake Station was located along the rail bed near the bridge just above the dam, while the Algonquin Hotel, built in 1908, was situated on the hill between the dam and the rail bed on the west side of the waterway.

Smoke Lake — KM 14.1

Nominigan Lodge formerly lay on the point on the north side of the large bay approximately one-third of the way down the east side of the lake. As an extra point of reference, the site is due north of Molly Island. The lodge was built in 1913 and accommodated guests who arrived at Algonquin Park Station on Cache Lake. A horse-drawn taxi would deliver visitors from the train station to the lodge for a dollar per person. The lodge was dismantled in 1977.

The main historic attraction is the remnants of a log chute on the creek on the east side of the portage between Smoke and Ragged lakes. This wooden chute, typical of those built throughout Algonquin from the mid-1800s to the early 1900s, was vital in transporting logs over damaging rapids and waterfalls. All that remains of this chute, built in 1896, is a scattering of rotten timbers and planks.

Rock Lake — eight kilometres south from KM 40.3

Access to the lake can be achieved from the boat launch near the T junction where Rock Lake Road meets the old railway bed, now used as the road to the campground. Alternately one could launch from the beach beside the Booth's Rock Trail parking lot.

Of particular interest are some Indian historical sites on the west side of the lake across from the campground. As you paddle along the west shore, heading south from where the Madawaska River enters the lake, you will come to a series of cottages. Just before the first cottage you will see an opening with foundations of a former building. Land here. If you walk north from the west edge of the clearing and parallel to the shoreline, you will soon enter a group of hemlocks (there may be orange flagging tape marking the route). Among the trees are a number of shallow pits, difficult to find because they are obscured by years of debris falling into them. These are known as "vision pits." The natives would lie in these small depressions, possibly for days on end, until they experienced a vision. Please do not disturb the site in any fashion.

While the pits may not be impressive to see, the rock piles that were erected in memory of the visions certainly are. To locate these climb the steep hillside in a southwesterly direction on about a 45-degree angle from the pits. Orange flagging tape may indicate the route to this site. After you have climbed for several minutes, you should reach a plateau below a second rise. Along this plateau are situated the moss-covered rock piles erected by the Indians.

The rail bed of the OA & PS Railway follows the eastern shoreline from the campground down to the large point about halfway along the east side of the lake. The remains of the Barclay Estate buildings, described earlier in **Other Historical Sites**, are found on this point, and the remnants of the large docks are visible on its south side.

On the west shore directly across from the point lies another historical Indian site. Indian pictographs were once visible on the cliff faces, but over time they have almost faded.

Sunday Creek — KM 42.7

Unlike the former routes, this one follows a winding creek to a couple of small lakes south of Highway 60. You can put in right from the highway, but it may be wise to park across the road in the Spruce Bog Board-walk parking lot.

Sunday Creek is a pretty, meandering creek that takes you to Norway and Fork lakes. At least two beaver dams block the creek, so be prepared to step out of the canoe and pull over them. Besides a close look at a bog and boreal forest along part of the route, you will also see the Visitor Centre on the ridge to the east of the creek.

Norway and Fork lakes are beautiful locations where you might come across moose. If you are here in late summer, be sure to try wolf howling along this route. Timber wolves travel through this area and will usually answer back.

Legend

MAJOR ROAD	HIKING TRAIL	PICNIC GROUND	MAMMAL VIEWING	CANOE ROUTE
SECONDARY ROAD	SKI TRAIL	CAMPGROUND	BIRD VIEWING	OUTFITTING
LOGGING ROAD	RIVER	HISTORIC SITE	WILDLIFE VIEWING	STORE
OLD RAILWAY	STREAM	SCENIC VIEW	PERMITS/INFORMATION	LODGE
	PARK BOUNDARY		$	PHONE

HIGHWAY
CORRIDOR
MAP 1

TEA LAKE

KM 8

WHISKEY RAPIDS TRAIL

WESTWARD LAKE

WESTERN UPLANDS BACKPACKING TRAIL

60

KM 3

KM 1

HERON LAKE

FEN LAKE SKI TRAIL

WEST GATE

$

OXTONGUE RIVER

SNOW LAKE

PARK (LONG) LAKE

Legend

═══ MAJOR ROAD	⋯⋯ HIKING TRAIL	🚐 PICNIC GROUND	🦫 MAMMAL VIEWING
═══ SECONDARY ROAD	⋯⋯ SKI TRAIL	⛰ CAMPGROUND	🦃 BIRD VIEWING
⋯⋯ LOGGING ROAD	〜 RIVER	🏛 HISTORIC SITE	🦉 WILDLIFE VIEWING
⋯⋯ OLD RAILWAY	— STREAM	✦ SCENIC VIEW	$ PERMITS/INFORMATION

CANOE ROUTE
OUTFITTING
STORE
LODGE

HIGHWAY CORRIDOR
MAP 2

JOE LAKE

SOURCE LAKE

MIZZY LAKE TRAIL

CANOE LAKE

PECK LAKE TRAIL

60

TANAMAKO LAKE

KM

HARDWOOD LOOKOUT TRAIL

SMOKE LAKE

TEA LAKE

KM 10

SWAN LAKE

RAGGED LAKE

HIGHWAY CORRIDOR
MAP 3

KEARNEY LAKE

WHITEFISH LAKE

POG LAKE

LAKE OF TWO RIVERS

PROVOKING LAKE

HIGHLAND BACKPACKING TRAIL

TWO RIVERS TRAIL

MEW LAKE

BAT LAKE TRAIL

JACK LAKE

HEMLOCK BLUFF TRAIL

TRACK AND TOWER TRAIL

CANISBAY LAKE

CACHE LAKE

TANAMAKOON LAKE

MINNESING SKI AND MOUNTAIN BIKE TRAIL

SOURCE LAKE

KM 38

KM 28

KM 21

60

28

MAJOR ROAD
SECONDARY ROAD
LOGGING ROAD
OLD RAILWAY

HIKING TRAIL
SKI TRAIL
RIVER
STREAM
PARK BOUNDARY

CANOE ROUTE
OUTFITTING
STORE
LODGE   PHONE

PICNIC GROUND   MAMMAL VIEWING
CAMPGROUND   BIRD VIEWING
HISTORIC SITE   WILDLIFE VIEWING
SCENIC VIEW   PERMITS/INFORMATION $

HIGHWAY
CORRIDOR
MAP 5

WHITEFISH
LAKE

COON LAKE

BOOTH'S
ROCK
TRAIL

ROCK
LAKE

PEN
LAKE

	MAJOR ROAD
	SECONDARY ROAD
	LOGGING ROAD
	OLD RAILWAY
	HIKING TRAIL
	RIVER
	STREAM
	PARK BOUNDARY
⌂	CAMPGROUND
	HISTORIC SITE
	MAMMAL VIEWING
	CANOE ROUTE
C	PHONE

IN MANY WAYS the eastern reaches are Algonquin's best-kept secret. Although busier in recent years, this portion of the park sees dramatically fewer visitors than the Highway 60 Corridor. Yet the East Side offers many of the same services available along Highway 60, including a public campground, interpretive trails and a number of access points to the Interior. The rugged landscape and coniferous forests give this side of the Park a distinctive beauty and "feel" quite different than that of the western uplands.

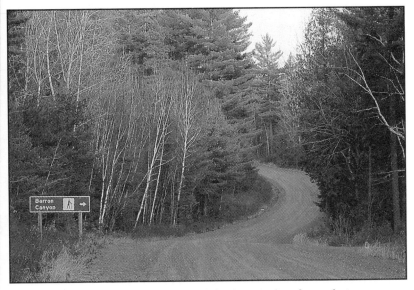

Algonquin's eastern reaches exhibit forests of poplar and pine.

Pine and poplar forests dominate the landscape, and a number of the plants and animals they support are either more common here or are not found on the West Side of the Park. Cardinal flower and poison ivy, both virtually unknown along the Highway Corridor, occur with some frequency here. This part of Algonquin offers excellent wildlife-viewing opportunities and many species, including white-tailed deer, moose, black bear and timber wolf, are frequently encountered. Whether you are here for one day or several, many historical as well as natural history sites can be reached with reasonable ease.

Access is achieved from Highway 17 just west of Pembroke at the first Petawawa exit. Turn south on Renfrew County Road 26 (opposite the airport sign). After travelling only 0.3 kilometre, turn right on Achray Road South (Renfrew County Road 28). This road is paved for the next nine kilometres. Starting from the point where the pavement ends, every kilometre is marked with a black-and-white sign. These markings continue to the end of public access at Lake Travers (72 kilometres farther along). Points of interest will be referenced in the same fashion as was done for the Highway Corridor. For example, the Sand Lake Gate lies just before the 18-kilometre marker, and its location will be given as KM 18.

There is a short access road leading to Mallard and Sec lakes at KM 15.2. You must purchase permits at the Sand Lake Gate if you wish to visit these lakes. As is the rule for all of Algonquin, travellers must have permits for either day, campground or Interior use. These can be purchased at the Sand Lake Gate.

From the gate the road extends another 54 kilometres to Lake Travers. There are two public access roads branching from Lake Travers Road, one at KM 24 (leading to McManus Lake) and another at KM 37.8 (leading to Achray on Grand Lake). You will also encounter a number of logging roads running off both sides of the main road; they are closed to public vehicular travel and are posted to that effect.

The roads inside this part of Algonquin are unpaved, so drive slowly. During dry periods they become quite dusty. Unless you enjoy a genuine "sandwich," you should prepare to roll up your windows when a cloud of dust from an approaching car draws near.

The East Side lacks gasoline and food services. Thus, you should make sure your vehicle is gassed up and that all of your food requirements are satisfied before you arrive. The Algonquin Portage Store is located 21 kilometres east of the Sand Lake Gate and offers meals, groceries, complete outfitting and gasoline.

INTERPRETIVE WALKING TRAILS

As along Highway 60, trail guides are available in dispensers at the beginning of the interpretive walking trails. They can also be purchased in advance from The Friends of Algonquin Park (address in the appendix **IMPORTANT SERVICES**).

Barron Canyon Trail — KM 28.9

The East Side boasts one of the most spectacular and unique trails in all of Algonquin, possibly eastern Canada. The Barron Canyon Trail visits, as its name suggests, a magnificent gorge along the Barron River. The trail, only 1.5 kilometres long, leads to the top of the canyon, 100 metres above the river.

This spot has always been one of my favourites in Algonquin. The rugged lichen-encrusted rocks of the canyon are part of the ancient Canadian Shield. Continual erosion and expansion of the canyon, largely caused by the actions of frost, is evidenced by the rock rubble known as talus slopes lying at the cliff bases. Far below the clifftop the Barron River appears as a tranquil ribbon of water. In earlier times, however, it was a raging glacial river flowing with the power of a thousand Niagaras. Long after the glaciers retreated farther north the icy water draining through here still maintained a cold environment in the canyon. Evidence of this is found not only in the types of plants growing on the cliff faces but also in the species of animals in the water below. Several types of northern plants, four kinds of cold-water crustaceans and one species of Arctic fish reside within the confines of the canyon, all relics of earlier populations.

A strange mixture of birds also makes its home here. Yellow-bellied Flycatchers, a boreal species, are common, as well as wetland-loving Common Yellowthroats. Red-tailed Hawks join Common Ravens and Turkey Vultures in soaring on thermals rising from the gorge. The soft trills of Dark-eyed Juncos join the abrupt inflections of Eastern Phoebes echoing throughout the canyon.

Besides supporting an interesting mixture of life, Barron Canyon offers breathtaking views. Because the trail visits the edge of a cliff make sure children and pets are under physical control when you are walking here.

Berm Lake Trail — five kilometres south from KM 37.8

The Berm Lake Trail begins at the end of the large parking area to your left as you approach the railway crossing at Achray.

This beautiful trail takes you around Berm Lake through a typical East Side pine forest. The ecology of this forest type is discussed in the trail guide.

With the fragrance of pines filling the air and carpets of lichens and mosses cushioning the rocks, the trail is a delight to walk. In early June pouches of pink lady's-slippers adorn the trail, adding yet another element of form and colour to the landscape.

This trail is part of the Achray trail system, and you may wish to extend your walk by taking one of the alternate loops. An excellent lookout lies along one section, and a scenic waterfall can be accessed by walking the longest section of trail (4.3 kilometres from the east end of Johnston Lake).

FACILITIES

Unlike the Highway Corridor, the East Side doesn't offer restaurants, lodges, outfitting services or interpretive facilities, although the Out-Side-In, a cabin at Achray formerly used by Tom Thomson, is slated for eventual use as an interpretive building. The Algonquin Portage Store, 21 kilometres outside the gate, offers outfitting and canoe shuttle services into this part of Algonquin.

PICNIC GROUNDS

The only formal picnic ground is situated on the Barron River at Squirrel Rapids (KM 20.3). There is also a parking lot for canoe trippers who launch from this site. Excellent places can be found at Achray to have lunch. Tables and barbecue stands are situated to the west of the stone building and boat launch. In addition, the drive-in camping site at Pretty Lake (KM 54.5) is a fine place to eat.

CAMPGROUNDS

The one campground on the entire East Side is situated at Achray, on Grand Lake. This is accessed by driving five kilometres south from KM 37.8. Of all the campgrounds in Algonquin this is one of the best-situated in terms of aesthetics. Grand Lake, as its name suggests, is one of the most exquisite lakes in all of Algonquin. Dramatic hills line the far side of the lake while extensive sand beaches border the campground shoreline. It is intriguing to think that Tom Thomson, who stayed in the log cabin between the stone office and the east pocket of the campground, admired and sketched the same sensational scenery that currently captivates us.

The campground lacks showers and laundry facilities but does have flush toilets. However, the superb beaches and splendid scenery more than make up for the absence of certain "conveniences."

The only drawback to this fine campground is that the Canadian National Railway has an active line running close to the campsites. The occasional train and steady hum of a generator at times compete with the choruses of Whip-poor-wills and wails of Common Loons.

Apart from canoeing to Interior campsites, one alternative exists to the campground at Achray. There is an Interior site on Pretty Lake (KM 54.5) that can be reached by car. In order to camp here, however, one must comply with the can-and-bottle ban, since this place is classified as an Interior site. Because the campsite lies directly beside Lake Travers Road, the noise from passing cars can be a drawback, although the racket generally dissipates after sunset.

WILDLIFE-VIEWING AREAS

Lake Travers Road offers many excellent opportunities for wildlife viewing. Most of Algonquin's larger animals are often seen along the 54 kilometres of road between the gate and Lake Travers. Certain species such as porcupine, black bear and white-tailed deer are more commonly encountered here than on the Park's West Side.

Most of the following animals can be found anywhere along Lake Travers Road. A few of the better locations for viewing each species is offered, and the chapter **OBSERVING WILDLIFE** offers tips that might increase your chances of finding these animals.

Moose

Moose can be seen between the gate and Lake Travers and are also occasionally observed along the road outside the Park. In June and early July, when moose are feeding on sodium-rich aquatic plants, the following waterways usually provide good viewing opportunities:

KM 21.4

The pond on the east side of the road is worth checking. There are a couple of short footpaths leading through the pines to the edge of the water.

KM 36.4

At this location you will find a dirt road leading off to the north (right). Although this road is closed to unauthorized vehicles, visitors are allow to walk it. About a half kilometre from Lake Travers Road lies a beautiful pond surrounded by picturesque dead trees.

Achray Trail System — five kilometres south of KM 37.8

From the Achray turn drive five kilometres until you reach the buildings at Achray. The Achray trail system begins at the far end of the large parking area to your left, just before the railway tracks. The Achray trail system consists of several loops that lead to various waterways. The Berm Lake Trail (4.3 kilometres) offers excellent views of Berm Lake. The boggy south end of the lake might present the best opportunities. The other section that might offer good moose viewing is the Johnston Lake loop.

KM 44

An excellent view of the west end of a small lake is offered from this location. Occasionally I have seen moose feeding here, particularly along the opposite shore.

KM 48.3

The large pond on the south side of the road is the best summer feeding spot for moose along this road. In late June as many as 12 moose have been seen at one time. A short path leads through the pines to a fine vantage point.

Pretty Lake — KM 54.5

As its name suggests, this is a scenic lake. Moose are sometimes seen feeding along the west side of the lake.

KM 56.5

The small pond on the east side of the road is one in which moose are frequently viewed. The road follows the edge of the pond on a sharp corner. While this corner offers an excellent view of the pond, it is a dangerous place to park. Be sure to pull off the road as far as you can in case another vehicle comes barrelling down the road, as they occasionally do. Arriving here shortly after sunrise will not only increase your chances of seeing moose but will also decrease the chances of being disturbed by other vehicles.

KM 69.4

Here you will find a road leading north. As is the case with all of the Park's "closed" roads, you are permitted to walk but not drive.

After walking a little over a kilometre through a pleasant jack pine forest, you will reach the large opening where a sawmill was formerly situated. A little farther along to your left will be a short road leading to a marsh in which moose feed.

KM 72

Moose occasionally feed in the pond on your left.

White-tailed Deer

White-tailed deer are frequently seen between the gate and the hydro line (KM 49.9), particularly in late spring and early summer. At sunrise deer often drink at the edges of ponds and streams. Thus, you might encounter them at some of the locations given above for moose. The hydro line and the abandoned mill site at Lake Travers (1.5 kilometres north from KM 69.4) are both good feeding areas.

Black bears are relatively common on this side of the Park.

Black Bear

Black bears are perhaps easiest to see along the road-side in late April and May when they are seeking out fresh grasses and sedges. I have had good luck in sighting these usually shy animals between KM 20 and KM 50, where the hydro line crosses. A few areas where bears might be more likely encountered include:

Achray Road — KM 37.8

In late evening or around dawn bears are occasionally seen on this five-kilometre road.

KM 40 to KM 43

This stretch of road frequently produces bears because a dump is situated nearby.

KM 45.9

The logging road leading south has been a good area for bears in the past. If you walk a short distance up it, you will arrive at a few open areas where berry-producing plants thrive. Bears frequently forage along this road.

Timber Wolf

I have found this part of Algonquin to offer the best opportunities to hear, and occasionally see, wolves. Several wolf packs have territories that include parts of Lake Travers Road. They regularly travel along the road through all seasons.

This habit of travelling provides us with important clues as to where to listen or howl. Wolf droppings are distinctive and stand out against the light colour of the sand. The droppings, also known as scats, are generally black and are full of their prey's hair. Fresh droppings look moist and won't be full of dirt from passing vehicles. On cold mornings extremely fresh scats have steam rising from them. On wet sand or fresh snow tracks are also a good clue to the presence of wolves. Whenever you encounter a fresh sign, try howling (refer to **OBSERV-ING WILDLIFE**). You may be rewarded for your efforts.

Over the years I have observed wolves at the following locations:

McManus Lake Road — KM 24

Try howling at this junction. Also try approximately four kilometres toward McManus Lake.

KM 30

Wolves frequently hunt in this vicinity and along the Barron River, just south of here.

Hydro Line — KM 49.9

The logging road that passes west of here is travelled by wolves, as are the roads situated below the hydro lines.

Pretty Lake — KM 54.5

This area has traditionally been good for locating wolves. I have fond memories of camping on this lake and having wolves respond from the far shore throughout the night. They also might be heard howling near Francis Lake, the lake just west of Pretty.

KM 61

A creek system lies just north where I have come across wolves a number of times.

KM 62 to KM 69

This section of road, which passes through the jack pine flats, has traditionally been one of the best wolf areas on the East Side and possibly in all of Algonquin. While you might encounter wolves anywhere along this stretch, KM 66 is the best place to stop. This point is the highest on the flats, and sound carries a phenomenally long distance to and from here.

Mill Site — 1.5 kilometres north of KM 69.4

This is another location worth trying.

Red Fox

Red foxes are usually easily located since they hunt along the roadsides, particularly at night. You might find rather tame foxes in a number of places along this route. Although the tameness is due to frequent contact with people, it is always best to be cautious and keep your distance.

KM 37.8

Since they often den near the turnoff to Achray, both adults and young are commonly seen in this vicinity from late April through summer. Foxes are frequently spotted along Achray Road, particularly the first kilometre south of the junction with Lake Travers Road.

KM 62 to KM 72

This stretch of road passes through a sandy plateau covered in jack pine. Excellent denning sites exist in the sandbanks throughout the area. In particular the stretch of road nearest Lake Travers often affords good viewing.

Mill Site — 1.5 kilometres north from KM 69.4

Another open sandy area where foxes not only hunt but also occasionally den.

Beaver

Lake Travers Road is excellent for observing beavers because many of the creeks and ponds along the road are occupied by these animals. Be aware, though, that beavers can, and do, change locations periodically. It may well be that after this book is published some of the sites described won't be occupied and that new ones might be. An active site will exhibit freshly cut sticks and newly placed mud on the dam or lodge. At the time of writing the following sites support active beaver colonies:

KM 21.4

The pond on the north side of the road is occupied by a colony.

Forbes Creek — KM 40

The creek crosses the road just 0.1 kilometre past this point. Beavers reside here and are occasionally seen from the road, particularly in spring.

KM 42.2 to 42.7

This stretch of Forbes Creek is worth checking.

KM 43.2

Scan for the familiar V of a beaver swimming across the lake. While spectacular sunsets are frequently viewed from this point, the next location along the lake is usually better for beaver observation.

KM 44

Beavers are commonly seen at this end of the lake in the evening.

KM 45.9

This pond was first colonized by beavers in 1992.

KM 48.3

Although this pond is better for moose viewing than for beaver watching, it is still worth checking.

KM 56.5

This pretty pond has an active beaver lodge directly in front of the small island with the broken-top pine.

KM 72

The beaver dam is an obvious structure right along the roadside.

Otter

Because otters and beavers frequent the same habitats, virtually any of the beaver locations could produce otters. Look at those sites in addition to the ones given below. Keep in mind that smaller creeks and larger lakes are used more frequently by otters than by beavers. Because otters range more widely than beavers, it is more difficult to predict where they might appear.

Otter activity varies seasonally. Early spring, when the ice is retreating from the waterways, and late fall are usually the best times for finding these agile animals. Some favoured otter viewing locations are:

Forbes Creek — KM 40.1

The creek crosses the road at this location and otters travel along it periodically.

KM 43.2

The bridge offers a good spot to scan both up and downstream for otters.

KM 44

An excellent view of this end of the lake is offered here.

Pretty Lake — KM 54.5

Otters regularly hunt the edges of this lake.

Lake Travers — 1.5 kilometres north from KM 69.4

Check the marsh on your left shortly after you reach the mill site. Also walk another few hundred metres to the point and carefully scan Lake Travers for these active animals.

Turtle Club Point (Lake Travers) — KM 72

For water access from the parking lot walk east on the footpath starting behind the bulletin board. This route takes you to a point where the magnificent Turtle Club lodge once stood. Only a few piles of rubble and five stark chimneys remain to mark the site of the buildings.

This point offers excellent views of the Petawawa River and the south end of Lake Travers. Otters hunt for fish and crayfish throughout the year here, but early spring and late fall are the best seasons to look. At these times the strong current keeps the water open at the mouth of the river while the lake remains frozen. Otters bring their catch onto the edge of the ice, using it as a dining table.

You should also check the pond on the south side of the road at KM 72. Just beyond the KM 72 sign, the bridge over the Petawawa offers another vantage point from which to look.

BIRDS

As in the section on birds in **THE HIGHWAY 60 CORRIDOR**, the northern species frequently sought by birders are detailed. In addition, a few locations for other species of interest are provided. Tips on locating particular species as well as attracting birds in general are given in **OBSERVING WILDLIFE**.

Spruce Grouse

While this bird is found in and near spruce bogs on the western side of Algonquin, on the East Side it is also found in jack pine forests. This species is actually more frequent here and is often observed, particularly at sunrise, picking grit from Lake Travers Road. Also, Spruce Grouse are commonly seen feeding in the pines along the road, especially in winter. If not seen on the road, they are sometimes discovered by walking through the jack pines. The following locations have consistently produced Spruce Grouse:

KM 61.5 to KM 62

The black spruce/tamarack bog on the south side of the road is worth checking.

KM 63 to KM 63.5

The south side of the road, particularly the black spruce edge, is a regular spot.

KM 65 to KM 70

Spruce Grouse are common throughout these jack pine flats. In particular the pines near the Stuart Spur junction at KM 67 and along the stretch between KM 67.5 and KM 69.4 usually harbour grouse.

North from KM 69.4

I have found Spruce Grouse on numerous occasions by walking the 1.5-kilometre road that leads north to the old mill site on Lake Travers.

Gray Jay

Gray Jays can be spotted on this side of the Park but, unlike the birds found along Highway 60, they lack coloured bands on their legs. However, they will still approach you for food, so be sure to have a chunk of bread or some other offering when you come across these gentle birds. Gray Jays are fairly common over much of this side of the Park, and a few of the more regular places for them are given here.

McManus Lake Road — KM 24

This eight-kilometre road frequently has Gray Jays at various points along it.

Barron Canyon Trail — KM 28.9

Gray Jays are regularly spotted along the trail, but the parking lot is as one of the better places to see them.

Achray Turn — KM 37.8

Gray Jays are often viewed at this junction.

Forbes Creek — KM 40.1

This boreal stretch commonly produces jays.

Pretty Lake — KM 54.5

Usually there is a family group not far from the campsite along the road.

KM 62.2

Anywhere near the creek is a good place to look for this species.

Whitson Creek — KM 63.7

This is one of the better spots for finding these and other northern birds.

The jack pine flats support a number of Gray Jays.

North from KM 69.4

The road to the mill site and the periphery of the open area, particularly near the marsh, usually has Gray Jays.

Black-backed Woodpecker

This northern woodpecker is frequently spotted on the East Side of Algonquin. I have encountered this species throughout most of this region, including along both interpretive trails and all along Lake Travers Road. Black-backed Woodpeckers might be found in any of the pine forests along this road. Some of the more regular locations for this bird include:

McManus Road — KM 24

One of the better spots on this generally good road is the black spruce bog that lies on the east (right) side of the road approximately one kilometre north of Lake Travers Road.

KM 35.2

The dead trees along the creek are worth checking.

KM 37

The wet spruce/fir area can be good for these northern birds.

Pretty Lake — KM 54.5

KM 61.5 to KM 62.2

Whitson Creek — KM 63.7

Although the area along the southeast side of the road is often productive, Black-backed Woodpeckers might be found anywhere near the creek.

OTHER SPECIES

Because of the pine/poplar forests certain species of birds are more easily found on this side of Algonquin than in the west. In particular Pine Warblers, Dark-eyed Juncos and Pileated Woodpeckers are quite common. A few additional species, including some of the East Side specialities, are discussed below.

Red Crossbill

Because of the abundance of white pines, their preferred seed tree, Red Crossbills are usually present year-round. Some years they occur in large numbers all along Lake Travers Road and frequently pick grit from its surface. In years of lower populations two relatively good spots are the Sand Lake Gate and the Turtle Club site east of KM 72. At the latter location Red Crossbills are often found gleaning lime from the chimneys, particularly during late fall through spring.

Merlin

These agile falcons are fairly common on the East Side. One pair usually resides near Achray and occasionally chases swallows near the boat launch.

The Lake Travers area usually supports several pairs of Merlins. They are frequently seen either perching on the tops of dead snags or flying over the jack pine flats, especially between KM 63 and KM 71.5. One pair usually nests at the old mill site (1.5 kilometres north of KM 69.4) and also hunts at the Turtle Club site (on the point east of the parking lot at KM 72).

Barred Owl

While perhaps not quite as common as they are along the Highway Corridor, Barred Owls can be heard on the East Side at a number of locations.

Barron Canyon Trail — KM 28.9

I have heard owls not only from the vicinity of the parking lot but also from the top of the trail.

KM 37

This is one of the traditional spots from where I have heard Barred Owls at night, particularly just before the break of dawn.

Maple Forest on Achray Road — 1.2 kilometres south from KM 37.8

This mature stand of hardwoods, one of the only stands along public roads on the East Side, invariably has a pair of Barred Owls residing in it.

Whip-poor-will and Common Nighthawk

Both of these birds are much more easily encountered on the East Side than along Highway 60. Nighthawks start hunting before dusk and are fairly easy to see. Their raspy *peent* and booming courtship sounds identify their whereabouts. Whip-poor-wills are also easy to hear but are generally much tougher to see. However, they frequently sit on sandy roads and their eyes glow bright red in headlight beams. Thus, a slow drive in the right areas might produce a view of these tough-to-see birds.

Both species can be heard at Grand Lake, but the best area lies in the jack pine flats between KM 64 and KM 67 (KM 66 is the optimal location). Try listening around dusk or just before sunrise.

OTHER HIGHLIGHTS

Because the topography and soils are different than those of western Algonquin, flora and fauna occur that are unique to the East Side. Several phenomena in particular are noteworthy.

A healthy population of wood turtles, a rare reptile throughout North America, exists along the Petawawa

River. These turtles are distinctive, possessing an ornate shell and orange front legs and throat. During the egg-laying season in early June, they are occasionally seen crossing Lake Travers Road near the lake of the same name. They are also seen along the Petawawa River. If you are fortunate enough to encounter a wood turtle, please don't disturb it. Another turtle found on this side of the Park and occasionally confused with wood turtles is Blanding's turtle. This species, however, has a bright yellow throat and smooth, spotted shell.

In late May and early June in even-numbered years the Macoun's Arctic, a boreal butterfly that appears every two years, flies in the larger jack pine stands near Lake Travers. It is pale orange and resembles a small washed-out monarch butterfly. Algonquin Park represents the southernmost range in Ontario of this butterfly.

Another noteworthy East Side phenomenon is the spectacular late summer show of wildflowers along the rivers, particularly at Poplar Rapids on the Petawawa River (KM 72.1). From late July to mid-August the edges of the Petawawa (and, in places, the Barron River) flame with the vibrant red blossoms of cardinal flower. The small island just upstream from the bridge over Poplar Rapids annually exhibits one of the most exquisite wildflower gardens I have ever seen. Here the soft pink of joe-pye weed, the yellow of grass-leaved golden-rod, the white of boneset and the crimson of cardinal flower all blend to create a symphony of colour.

HISTORICAL POINTS OF INTEREST

The East Side of Algonquin was one of the first to feel the logger's axe because of the rich supply of pines that grew here and also because of its closeness to the Ottawa Valley, the hub of lumbering activity in eastern Ontario. The Petawawa River was extremely important in the transport of logs from the Park to the Ottawa River, and every spring swarms of men moved thousands of logs down its length. The last log drive in Algonquin Park took place on this river in 1959.

Because of its rugged beauty this side of Algonquin also attracted the attention of renowned artists. Tom Thomson not only sketched some of his most famous works on the East Side but also worked here as a fire ranger in the summer of 1916.

Logging Camp Remains — KM 31.6

A boggy pond lies on the south side of the road. On the northwest side of this wetland you will find the remnants of a logging camp, which was built in the 1930s by a contractor for the Whitmore Lumber Company. An old well, foundations and assorted camp debris are present. The ruins of an older camp, probably a camboose, are also located here.

Pine Forest Research Area — KM 36.4

A research project on the dynamics of white pine growth was conducted here in 1929. A joint venture between the Department of Lands and Forests (now the Ministry of Natural Resources) and the University of Toronto, the study was the first of its kind in Ontario. Trees bearing numbered tags from this program can be found in proximity to the junction of Lake Travers Road and the logging road running north. The trees were measured again in 1949, but no further examination occurred until the 1980s.

Stone Building at Achray — five kilometres south from KM 37.8

As you enter Achray, a large stone building lies directly across the railway tracks. The building, erected in 1933 as an office for this part of Algonquin, was constructed with stone hauled from across the lake. It continues to be used as the headquarters for the East Side.

This stone building is still used as the headquarters for the eastern side of the Park.

The Out-Side-In Cabin — Achray

This structure, used as a fire ranger's cabin in the early 1900s, is located just east of the stone building. Tom Thomson lived here in the summer of 1916 when he worked as a fire ranger. During his stay, he painted a sign bearing this unusual name. Unfortunately the original sign's whereabouts are currently unknown, but a replica is to be erected on the cabin.

Site of Tom Thomson's *The Jack Pine* — Grand Lake

Tom Thomson's famous painting was sketched in 1916 from a point just south of the Achray Campground. To reach this site travel along the road through the east end of the campground until you come to a small parking lot. From here continue by foot along the road through a chain gate and across a short causeway. If this part of the road is underwater, as it can be at times, you can skirt around it by travelling along the railway tracks to your left. The road continues through woods and eventually arrives at a large expanse of beach. Just as you arrive at the beach, climb onto the rocky hill on your immediate right. When you stand on the top of this rocky knoll, face the delightful rolling hills surrounding Carcajou Bay, southwest across the lake. The jack pine is gone, but the rolling hills that appear in the painting's background easily identify this as the site of the famous work of art.

Ranke Sawmill Site and Log Chute — 0.4 kilometre north of KM 38.3

Walk up the road leading north from Lake Travers Road. A short distance in you will reach a gravel pit around which remnants of the Ranke Sawmill are situated. This mill was built, as many mills and logging camps were, on the site of a much older camp.

Just beyond the pit is Forbes Creek. Walk downstream approximately 100 metres or less to a small rapids. The flat planks along the creek are from the bottom of a log chute that once carried logs past these rapids.

Stuart's Spur — 0.5 kilometre south from KM 67

Stuart was the manager of the Pembroke Shook Mills, which built a loading spur — a short section of rail — here in 1929. At this spur joining the Canadian National Railway pine logs were loaded onto flatcars by a steam hoist. The high ground around the small parking area just north of Travers Creek once held a number of buildings, including a stable, blacksmith shop, cookery and bunkhouses. The alder flats between the high ground and the railway tracks was the holding area for pine logs destined for the shook mills in Pembroke. (Shooks were prefab wooden boxes.) A dam on Travers Creek kept the holding area flooded to prevent logs from staining due to exposure to the air before they were loaded for transport. The camp lasted until 1954.

A more recent camp was run by Shaw Lumber on the opposite side of the railway tracks near the large clearing. In order to transport the logs from this site the railway spur was moved to that side of the tracks. High quality red pine logs had their bark peeled before they were shipped for use as telephone, hydro or utility poles. Lower-grade red and white pine logs were shipped directly to the Pembroke Shook Mills. This camp shut down in the late 1960s but was briefly opened for the 1980-81 season. In 1988 the camp was completely dismantled and the spur area planted.

Don't be surprised if you see horse hoof prints or even horses on this road. Access by this method is allowed along the road to White Partridge Lake.

Pembroke Lumber Company Mill Site — 1.5 kilometres north from KM 69.4

Park safely off the main road and walk 1.5 kilometres north along the side road to a large opening, the site of a mill run by the Pembroke Lumber Company. Built in the early 1930s, it ran until 1977, a phenomenal length of time for an isolated mill in Algonquin. Not much remains today except for debris scattered here and there. The most obvious remaining structure is a small water tower to your left when you approach the lake.

Radio Observatory — KM 71.5

This area was set aside in 1959 for the National Research Council of Canada (NRC). A large radio telescope, known as the "big dish," is located on the private road to the west. It can be partially viewed from KM 72 behind the pond. Banks of smaller dishes are located throughout the research area, and one bank is visible along the road to the CN railway station (west from KM 70.3). The dishes were used to detect radio signals from outer space. Last operated by the NRC in the late 1980s, this complex is now used by the Institute for Space and Terrestrial Science.

Turtle Club Site — 0.2 kilometre north from KM 72

Park in the lot for water access to the lake and look for the footpath that starts from behind the information board. The path leads to the point where the Turtle Club was situated. Erected in 1933, the club was a private lodge owned by the family of J. R. Booth, the famous lumber baron. Five chimneys plus a pile of debris mark the site where the unique structure formerly stood. The elegant log building was constructed in the shape of a turtle, Booth's bark mark (a symbol inscribed on the side of logs to identify the owner). Purchased by the government in 1973, the building was dismantled five years later.

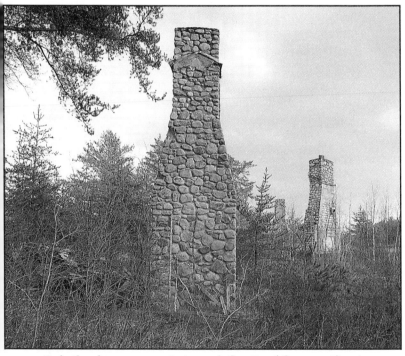

Only the chimneys remain to mark the site of the magnificent Turtle Club.

Glance Piers — KM 72.1

If you stand on the bridge over Poplar Rapids and look upstream, you will see piers of piled rocks jutting into the Petawawa River. Probably built well before the turn of the century, these rock piles kept logs away from the shoreline and directed them into the channel during spring river drives. For over 100 years the Petawawa River carried logs from Algonquin Park to the Ottawa River. The last log drive in the Park took place on this river in 1959.

Canoeing on the East Side

Although fewer in number, the canoe routes here are often more dramatic than those in the Highway Corridor. Another major difference is that fabulous white-water canoeing is available for those who seek it. The Petawawa River is renowned for this feature, but only people with experience should attempt to shoot the rapids. Some parts of the Petawawa are extremely hazardous, and skilled canoeists have perished while trying to shoot them. *The Canoe Routes of Algonquin Provincial Park* map brochure details the location of the rapids and the portages that allow you to bypass them. A detailed guide to Petawawa white-water canoeing is scheduled for publication by The Friends of Algonquin Park in 1993.

Available Services

There are no rental services on the East Side. However, the Algonquin Portage Store, which is 21 kilometres outside the gate, offers complete outfitting and shuttle services.

Recommended Short Trips

The following are all short excursions, one day or less, that could be extended into longer trips if desired. Remember, cans and bottles are prohibited in the

Interior and camping permits are required for overnight stays. The *Canoe Routes of Algonquin Provincial Park* map brochure is essential for any canoe trip in the Park.

Barron River

The 100-metre-high cliffs of Barron Canyon make canoeing the Barron River an awe-inspiring event. The river can be accessed from Squirrel Rapids (KM 20.3) or from the Brigham Access (KM 33.2). Both sites have parking facilities. The Brigham Access is closer to the canyon but has a steeper access to the water. From Squirrel Rapids to the canyon you are paddling against the gentle current, but on the return trip you are, not surprisingly, travelling with it. One enjoyable way of doing this route is to travel in two parties. One vehicle can be dropped off at Squirrel Rapids, making the trip a one-way excursion from the Brigham Access.

The Barron Canyon is as impressive from below as it is from the trail at the top.

When you journey through the canyon, you are travelling back in time. Birds that usually nest on man-made structures can be seen nesting on these cliffs as they have done for countless thousands of years. When you paddle along the sheer wall of rock, watch for the mud nests of Barn Swallows cemented under overhangs at about eye level. Flowing streams of excrement below the nests identify their location. As you near active nests, the adult birds noisily dive-bomb your canoe. Eastern Phoebes, less aggressive birds, also share the same recesses, but their nests have more moss and lichen components than those of Barn Swallows.

Higher up on the cliff faces, the bulky stick nests of Common Ravens can also be seen. From the tops of the cliffs Red-tailed Hawks indignantly scream at your intrusion into their domain.

The cliff faces are also adorned with a variety of intriguing plants. Plants from the far north remain as tokens of the cold past. Many thrive here because of the lime that percolates from rock crevices. Because lime is rare throughout most of Algonquin, a number of the plants you pass by are unique to the canyon. The lichen *Xanthoria* is responsible for the beautiful orange that carpets much of the exposed rock. Another plant to look for is the encrusted saxifrage, easily identified because of the white dots of lime exuded around the periphery of the leaves, which grow in a basal rosette.

The roar of the river is now silenced, as is the thunder of log drives that occurred here in more recent times. The Barron River was an important route for spring drives, and countless thousands of logs passed through here from the mid-1800s to the early 1900s. The grave of one unfortunate driver lies along the river at the second campsite below the canyon, hidden by a clump of conifers.

Along the river you will find old logs left behind from these drives. Check the ends carefully for the log stamp of J. R. Booth, the great lumber baron who brought the OA & PS Railway to Algonquin. The stamp was a diamond with the initials J.R. inside it.

The indistinct ruins of a log chute can be found at Cache Rapids, the first set of rapids upstream from Squirrel Rapids.

Grand Lake

Despite the presence of motorboats (up to 10-horsepower motors are allowed), Grand Lake remains a marvellous body of water to paddle. Several options exist as to where you can go and what you can see on a day's paddle from Achray, five kilometres south from KM 37.8.

Option 1 — Grand Lake.   A full day can be spent paddling to the lake's northwest extremity and back. I would allow a minimum of eight hours for this, so you should start at dawn to ensure plenty of time for exploring.

With its narrow configuration Grand Lake is more like a river than a lake. Two points of interest lie along this route. Approximately halfway up the lake, on the west side, is the portage to Wenda Lake. Discarded mechanical items and an old root cellar can be found near the start of the portage. These identify the site of a former lumber camp.

The remains of the McLachlin Depot, a central supply settlement for lumbering operations in the area, are located at the north end of the large bay at the northeast corner of the lake. At one time logs were hauled overland on wooden rails by a steam locomotive with double-flange wheels, then deposited in Grand Lake.

At the very top end of the lake lies one of the few cattail marshes in Algonquin. Here Great Blue Herons and American Bitterns stalk frogs along the narrow creek that meanders through the marsh. If you are fortunate, you might startle a Virginia Rail into uttering its alarm call, a weird *wugh-wugh-wugh-wugh-wugh* that sounds like a giant coin wobbling to a halt after being spun on a tabletop. These secretive birds also emit a sharp *dik-dik-kidik-kidik*. The Grand Lake marsh supports the highest density of Virginia Rails in the Park.

Across the logging road at the north end of the marsh lies Clemow Lake, the beautiful body of water depicted in the coniferous forest diorama in the Algonquin Visitor Centre. A lumber camp formerly stood at the north end of this lake at the site of the northernmost campsite.

Option 2 — Carcajou Bay. Carcajou is a French word that means "wolverine." Although these large weasels are not currently known in the Park, the use of this word in naming a bay, a lake and a creek suggests that perhaps at one time they were here.

It is the hills from the bay region that form the backdrop for Tom Thomson's *The Jack Pine*, painted from the Achray side. The route is a beautiful one that should be done well after black fly season ends. The East Side is notoriously bad for these biting creatures during June, and the Carcajou area seems to hold the highest population in the world!

After leaving Achray, a relatively short paddle brings you across the lake. Before entering the bay you pass by an island with a Herring Gull colony on it. At times the gulls have an intriguing method of nest defence — they fly over your canoe and either vomit rotting fish or defecate on you. Thus, I suggest you give the island a wide berth.

Once in the "safety" of the bay carefully check the rocks on your right (the north side). Indian pictographs are situated just above eye level on the low cliffs immediately after you enter the bay. These are quite faded but still discernible. I have found that by splashing water on them the symbols become more visible.

The dramatic rocky hills bordering Carcajou Bay make this a particularly enjoyable route. A delightful waterfall is situated at the south end of the bay. After one short portage, you have the choice of taking another short portage and canoeing into Lower Spectacle Lake or continuing up McDonald Creek, a winding bog-lined waterway and an excellent moose area in the summer.

Option 3 — Stratton Lake.   After leaving Achray, paddle along the south shore of the lake, past the extensive sand beaches where native people once camped. Soon after entering the narrows you will reach a short portage skirting the dam. Stratton Lake lies on the far side of the portage. It is is a beautiful rock-bound body of water that seems more like a narrow river than an actual lake. Ospreys and otters are frequently seen as they search for fish in the clear waters. Since this was an important waterway for log drives in earlier years, evidence of that activity abounds.

Once at the south end of the lake you have the choice of taking a 45-metre portage into St. Andrew's Lake or paddling to the end of the bay that runs north from here. I would suggest you do both, but obviously not at the same time! High Falls, a thundering waterfall, lies at the end of the north-running bay, and the remains of a logging camp are situated on the extreme northern tip.

St. Andrew's Lake provides access to a couple of fascinating relics from early logging days. A pointer boat, a logging vessel narrowed at both ends, lies at the bottom of the lake at its northern extremity, just before the portage and closer to the far shore. If the water surface is not ruffled by wind, you should be able to see it by peering into the water.

Another fascinating bit of history lies along the portage into Highfalls Lake. The remnants of the wooden log chute used to transport logs around the rapids along the portage are still apparent. The best section lies between the pond approximately halfway along the portage and the end of the portage at Highfalls Lake.

Because the chute lies on the far side of the rapids, which the portage parallels, you may wish to walk along that side to view it. After you finish the portage to Highfalls Lake, you can paddle to the opposite shore and walk back up the rapids.

From here, if time permits, you can travel on to Barron Canyon, but several small portages must be traversed to get there. If two parties are involved, one vehicle could be left at either Brigham Access or Squirrel Rapids. Be sure if you do a one-way trip that you start early in the day to avoid paddling in the dark.

The ruins of an early logging camp can be seen along the portage between Opalescent and Ooze lakes, and the remains of a cabin, possibly a river drivers' shelter, lie halfway along the 285-metre portage between Ooze and The Cascades.

Lake Travers

This, my favourite lake in Algonquin, offers excellent canoeing. However, on windy days Travers can be rough, so keep abreast of the weather situation while on it.

There is a parking lot and boat launch at KM 72. Here you launch directly into the Petawawa River. As you paddle along, you are following the route of the early river drivers. The point on your right bearing tall chimneys is the site of the Turtle Club, described in **Historical Points of Interest** in this chapter.

If you paddle east around the south edge of the lake, you will pass by the residences for the Space Research Institute. Beyond these houses lies an interesting marsh. Here you will likely see Great Blue Herons and American Bitterns. At daybreak the marsh is full of life. I have seen deer, raccoons, moose, muskrats, otters and beavers in this spot.

From here you paddle north past the old mill site with the remnants of a dock and other buildings along the rocky point. Beyond there lies a shallow bay with a long sand beach. Farther north the scenery becomes more dramatic as steep hills embrace the lake where it narrows back into a river.

The large island just before the narrows is a moose-calving spot in mid-May and usually harbours nesting Merlins. A point bearing an old logging camp lies about half a kilometre beyond the small island and campsites in the narrows. The site is on the west side of the river and is hidden by alders. About another three kilometres past this you will see that the hillside to the right of you has had most of the trees knocked down. This blowdown occurred during a windstorm in 1983. Just beyond that spot lies the portage around Big Thomson Rapids. Remnants of a wooden logging dam are quite evident near the start of the portage. Unless you are planning to continue down the Petawawa on an overnight excursion, this portage will be the place where you turn back.

McManus, Smith and Whitson lakes

These so-called lakes are simply widenings in the Petawawa River. To access McManus take the well-marked road at KM 24. The parking lot and water access lie eight kilometres from the turn.

On the first leg of this trip you paddle against a gentle current. There are only two small portages along the route, the first a mere 90 metres in length. If the water is high enough and you have the strength, the first portage can be bypassed by paddling up the rapids. But believe me, this is tough work and the portage is a considerably easier option.

While these lakes offer pleasant canoeing, the landscape is less varied than along the other routes. This route does, however, have some interesting tree species. Along the shores one finds green alder, a much rarer shrub in the Park than its abundant relative, speckled alder. Green alder has sticky young leaves and branchlets, and the conelike catkins are held on long stalks. Speckled alders have dry leaves and branchlets and short-stalked catkins.

On the small islands in Whitson Lake silver maple will also be found. This southern tree is quite rare in Algonquin except along the Petawawa River. The leaves of this maple are very deeply cut in contrast to those of its relatives. From the islands the rising song of Warbling Vireos, a southern species irregular and rare elsewhere in the Park, can be heard.

The return trip is virtually effortless, since you are travelling with the current all the way.

EAST SIDE
MAP 8

WHITSON LAKE

SMITH LAKE

McMANUS LAKE

MAJOR ROAD
SECONDARY ROAD
LOGGING ROAD
RAILWAY LINE
HIKING TRAIL
RIVER
STREAM
PARK BOUNDARY
PICNIC GROUND
CAMPGROUND
HISTORIC SITE
SCENIC VIEW
MAMMAL VIEWING
BIRD VIEWING
WILDLIFE VIEWING
CANOE ROUTE
PERMITS/INFORMATION

EAST SIDE
MAP 9

Legend:
- —— MAJOR ROAD
- —— SECONDARY ROAD
- ·—·—· LOGGING ROAD
- +—+—+ RAILWAY LINE
- ⊃⊃⊃ CANOE ROUTE
- ······· HIKING TRAIL
- ~~~ RIVER
- ~~ STREAM
- ·—··—·· PARK BOUNDARY
- ········· HYDRO LINE

- 🍗 PICNIC GROUND
- △ CAMPGROUND
- 🏛 HISTORIC SITE
- ✦ SCENIC VIEW
- 🦫 MAMMAL VIEWING
- 🐦 BIRD VIEWING
- 🦌 WILDLIFE VIEWING
- $ PERMITS/INFORMATION

KM 28

KM 38

KM 45

BARRON CANYON TRAIL

BARRON RIVER

HIGHFALLS LAKE

FORBES CREEK

BERM LAKE

ACHRAY TRAIL SYSTEM

JOHNSTON LAKE

STRATTON LAKE

GRAND LAKE

EAST SIDE
MAP 12

FRANCIS LAKE

PRETTY LAKE

DEPOT CREEK

FORBES CREEK

WHITSON CREEK

KM 42

KM 50

KM 58

KM 64

—— MAJOR ROAD	······· HIKING TRAIL
—— SECONDARY ROAD	∿∿ RIVER
—··— LOGGING ROAD	∿∿ STREAM
—+—+— RAILWAY LINE	—··— PARK BOUNDARY
⌒⌒ CANOE ROUTE	········· HYDRO LINE

🎪 PICNIC GROUND	🦌 MAMMAL VIEWING
⛺ CAMPGROUND	🦅 BIRD VIEWING
🏛 HISTORIC SITE	🔭 WILDLIFE VIEWING
🔭 SCENIC VIEW	$ PERMITS/INFORMATION

EAST SIDE
MAP 13

LAKE
TRAVERS

P E T A W A W A   RIVER

KM 70

KM 66

	MAJOR ROAD		HIKING TRAIL		PICNIC GROUND		MAMMAL VIEWING
	SECONDARY ROAD		RIVER		CAMPGROUND		BIRD VIEWING
	LOGGING ROAD		STREAM		HISTORIC SITE		WILDLIFE VIEWING
	RAILWAY LINE		PARK BOUNDARY		SCENIC VIEW		PERMITS/INFORMATION
	CANOE ROUTE		HYDRO LINE				

THE BASIN DEPOT AREA possesses a long history of logging and sparse settlement. Logging began in the Bonnechere Valley before 1830. The Bonnechere River, which the road roughly parallels, was previously used for log transport during spring drives. In the summer months this meandering waterway becomes more of a creek and, for much of its length, isn't traversable by canoe. Basin Depot, a supply base and stopover spot for lumbermen, was the centre of logging activity between the mid-1800s and 1913. One of the buildings, repaired in recent years by the Algonquin Forestry Authority, is the oldest building in the Park.

Basin Road is unpaved and stretches 25 kilometres from the Park boundary to the end of public access at the hydro line. There are two short side branches to Basin and Foys lakes. Although there are no facilities along this road, the area is still worth visiting for the wildlife and historical sites. Every kilometre of main road is marked with kilometre signs, as is the case along the Highway Corridor and Lake Travers Road.

The marking system for this road begins at the intersection with a north-leading road two kilometres west of Turner's Camp. The Park boundary lies 8.5 kilometres west of this junction, halfway between the KM 8 and KM 9 markers. This will be designated as KM 8.5. Basin Depot is situated at KM 14.2.

Access to this part of Algonquin is achieved by travelling west on Turner's Road from Highway 62, just north of the entrance into Bonnechere Provincial Park. Turner's Road is approximately 40 kilometres west of Pembroke.

The Basin Depot region supports pine and poplar forests that are representative of the entire northeastern two-thirds of the Park. In addition, jack pines are prevalent in several areas, particularly near the Park boundary and in the vicinity of the hydro line. These forests support a variety of wildlife, including a large population of white-tailed deer and beaver. In turn these animals support several packs of timber wolves, which are often heard at the appropriate times of year.

There are no campgrounds in this part of Algonquin, but drive-in camping is available at Bonnechere Provincial Park, only 16 kilometres southeast of the Park boundary. Permits purchased at Bonnechere Provincial Park are valid as day-use permits for Algonquin. Day-use and Interior camping permits can be obtained at Turner's Camp, which lies 4.6 kilometres west of Highway 62 and 10.5 kilometres east of the Park boundary. There are two Interior campsites at the western extremity of the road. One is situated on a pretty little lake at KM 31.1. However, to camp here you not only need an Interior permit but you must also heed the can-and-bottle ban in effect for the Park Interior.

WILDLIFE-VIEWING AREAS

Because the forest type is similar to that on the East Side of Algonquin, many of the same plants and animals are found in the Basin Depot area. The road passes by several ponds and other small waterways that present opportunities to view animals such as otters and beavers. Porcupines are relatively common due to the abundance of poplars. A few of the better spots for specific animals are given below. The chapter **OBSERVING WILDLIFE** provides suggestions for finding these and other animals.

Moose

Although they might be encountered anywhere along the road, moose are seen more regularly in early summer when feeding on the sodium-rich aquatic plants in waterways along the road. A few of the better locations are given here.

- Pond — KM 19.5.
- Pond — KM 27.6. This has traditionally been one of the "hot spots" for moose.
- Wetland — KM 30.8.
- Pond and creek — KM 31.1.
- Bonnechere River — KM 32.2.

White-tailed Deer

The entire area is good for deer. Thus, they might be encountered anywhere along the road. The large openings around Basin Depot (KM 14.2) are usually productive.

Black Bear

Another animal that might be seen anywhere along the main road, black bears frequently forage along the hydro line at the northern extremity of Basin Road.

Timber Wolf

This road transects one of the better areas for wolf activity because of the abundance of deer and beavers, their principal prey. When fresh signs (i.e., tracks or scats) are encountered along the road, howling attempts (see **OBSERVING WILDLIFE**) should be made.

In particular, try the following locations:

- Basin Depot — KM 14.2.
- Foys Lake turn — KM 23.6.
- Hydro line — KM 33.6.

Beaver

Beavers are quite common along this road. At the time of writing the following waterways are occupied by beavers:

- KM 10.1.
- KM 19.5.
- One kilometre north from KM 23.6 (Foys Lake turn).
- KM 26.
- KM 27.6.
- KM 29.6.
- KM 30.8.

Otter

Because otters travel widely their whereabouts are not as predictable as those of beavers. However, they are frequently encountered in ponds and creeks along Basin Road. Any of the locations for beavers and moose might produce otters. In addition, the creek along the north side of the road from KM 20.8 to KM 21 is particularly good for otter activity.

BIRDS

The pine and poplar forests support birds similar to those on the East Side. Gray Jays are often viewed along Basin Road, as are Black-backed Woodpeckers, another northern species. Pileated Woodpeckers are also quite common.

Gray Jay and Black-backed Woodpecker

Because of the prevalence of northern coniferous forests around wetlands along Basin Road, both these northern birds are fairly common. While they may be encountered almost anywhere, there are a few locations that may offer better opportunities in seeing one or both species.

- Park Boundary — KM 8.5.
- Basin Depot — KM 14.2.
- KM 21.6.
- KM 24 to KM 26.
- KM 30.8 to KM 31.1.
- Bonnechere River — KM 32.2.

HISTORICAL POINTS OF INTEREST

Because of early settlement and the area's importance to the logging industry, Basin Road is richly endowed with historical sites. The earliest settlers were deemed "squatters" when Algonquin Park expanded to include this area in 1914. Their land was taken over and the families were ousted at that time, since they didn't hold formal title.

Basin Road — KM 8.5 to KM 14.4

The present road generally follows the original Basin Road that ran from Eganville to Basin Depot, situated just beyond KM 14. Built in the mid-1800s, Basin Road was an important supply route to the depot that serviced all the logging operations in this area.

In 1967 Martin Garvey, a homesteader's son raised only a few kilometres past the boundary, recollected that in 1909 this road was incredibly busy as a supply route for lumbering operations. As many as 40 teams of horses would pass along this road from 4:00 p.m. until dark. Over the entire day many more teams would have travelled the road.

McDonald Grave — KM 11.2

This grave is marked by a white cross and picket fence. James McDonald cleared the area for farming sometime in the mid- to late 1800s. Alexander McDonald, the infant son of Ronald, a brother of James, was buried here in 1888. The inscription on the cross is still legible. The McDonalds lived on the farm until the provincial government took it over in 1914.

This area was once known as Sligo, after the county in Ireland where Paddy Garvey, another early settler, was born. Sometime after 1855 Garvey set up Sligo House, a stopping place for lumbermen, just south of here along the Bonnechere. After 1870 Garvey concentrated on farming at the next site.

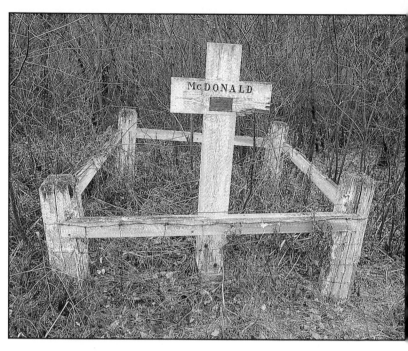

The McDonald Grave is testament to the trying conditions that early homesteaders faced.

Garvey's Homestead — KM 12.5

Paddy Garvey, who ran Sligo House, farmed here from about 1870 to 1914. As was the case with other "squatters" like the McDonald family, he was uprooted when the Park expanded.

Basin Depot — KM 14.2 to KM 14.4

This open area with two standing buildings has a long and interesting history. The site was important as a central supply and stopover place for lumbermen because it was situated at the junction of two main supply routes. One ran north from Basin Creek to Grand Lake. The other ran parallel to the Bonnechere River to a depot at White Partridge Lake and through to Radiant Lake.

This log building is the oldest structure still standing in the Park.

While the exact date of the first building is unknown, in 1843 four shanties were present. By 1890 there were 10 buildings, including a blacksmith shop, a post office and the Basin House, a large building containing a men's bar and living quarters. Between 1949 and 1960 the depot was run by Shoosplin Woods Limited. During this time, 18 buildings stood here and the depot employed 98 men. A ranger cabin, built around the turn of the century, was removed in the 1970s.

The small log building at KM 14.2 was constructed in 1892 by the McLachlin Lumber Company. Originally built as an office, it served as a hospital during a diphtheria epidemic that same year. In 1909 it was used again as an office by the John D. McRae Lumber Company. After the ownership transferred at least two more times, the structure was employed as a school from 1911 to 1913. The cabin has also served as a harness shop and a summer residence and is the oldest building still standing in Algonquin Park.

Along the east bank of Basin Creek on either side of Basin Road lie two graves enclosed in white picket fences. It is believed that these graves belong to rivermen who drowned during an 1895 spring log drive along the Bonnechere. However, other reports suggest they are graves either of Depot residents or victims of the 1892 diphtheria outbreak.

On the west side of Basin Creek is a large building that was apparently built by the McLachlin Lumber Company. After 1940 it served as a warehouse and storage facility for the Department of Lands and Forests (now the Ministry of Natural Resources). The graves of victims from the 1892 diphtheria outbreak are reportedly located in the poplar grove behind this building.

CANOEING IN THE BASIN DEPOT AREA

Unfortunately this area is not well endowed with canoeing possibilities. The Bonnechere River is generally only traversable in the northern section, which is best accessed either at KM 32.2 or at the end of the road at the hydro line. Along much of its length the Bonnechere is a winding, marshy waterway, more like a creek than a river. Great Blue Herons, Black Ducks, moose and otters frequent this river.

Basin and Foys lakes are the only sizable bodies of water in the area. Both have access roads that can be rough to travel at times.

IN ADDITION to the three main access areas previously profiled (Highway Corridor, East Side and Basin Depot), Algonquin Park can also be entered at a number of other points. Most of these are used primarily for canoe access to the vast Interior and offer few services apart from a permit office and a parking area. However, three of the entrances do have small drive-in campgrounds. These three plus one other will be briefly discussed here. Information concerning the remaining access points is detailed in the *Canoe Routes of Algonquin Provincial Park* map brochure available at all retail outlets in the Park, or by mail from The Friends of Algonquin Park (address provided in the appendix **IMPORTANT SERVICES**).

The majority of the access points are used to start longer canoe trips into the Park Interior. With over 1,500 kilometres of possible routes the Park Interior holds a vast number of both historical and natural history sites. The discussion of all of the known places would require a massive book (or books) and is beyond both the scope and intent of this guide. Only a brief listing of a few of the Interior highlights will be provided, following the brief overview of each access point.

BRENT

Situated on beautiful Cedar Lake along the Petawawa River, Brent is the most developed access point in the northern part of Algonquin. There is an outfitting and supply store and a small drive-in campground with only basic facilities (i.e., no flush toilets or showers). The road into Brent, stretching 40 kilometres from Deux-Rivières on Highway 17, is extremely rough and requires slow driving.

At present Brent is a mere shadow of its former self. In earlier years it was a thriving summer recreational and lumbering community. While the railway line is still in use, the lodge it brought tourists to is no longer present. Also gone is the sawmill that was the heart of the lumbering industry here.

Apart from access to Cedar Lake and the Petawawa River, the other highlight of the region is the Brent Crater Trail. This is the only interpretive trail in the northern part of the Park. It visits the crater formed when a meteorite crashed here about 450 million years ago.

The trail leads to the bottom of the crater where evidence of the impact, such as shattered rock, can be seen. The trail guide discusses the clues that reveal the origin of the crater. One interesting aspect is that limestone, a rare rock type in Algonquin, is present here. These deposits allow the growth of calcareous plants that are otherwise rare in Algonquin. Some of these, such as bulb-let bladder fern, can be found along the trail. A lookout tower on the southeast rim of the crater affords a view of the opposite rim four kilometres away.

Permits and a few publications are sold at the Park office located at the junction with Wendigo Lake Road 24 kilometres before Brent. Motorboats with a maximum 20-horsepower motor are allowed on Cedar Lake.

KIOSK

Kiosk is located on Kioshkokwi Lake, 48 kilometres southwest of Mattawa on Highway 17. Highway 630, the 30.4-kilometre access road from Highway 17, is paved.

At one time Kiosk was a busy town with a sawmill, school and numerous residents. The sawmill, built in

1936, burnt down in 1973 and was rebuilt outside the Park. With the heart of the community gone the families left one after the other. At the time of writing only one family still resides here, making this once-thriving community virtually a ghost town.

The office is at the lake, just past the railway tracks (this is the same active railway line that passes through Brent and Achray). Permits are sold here as well as a few publications. The small campground offers only basic facilities. Just west of the office lies a log building used formerly as a ranger cabin. Motorboats with a maximum of 20-horsepower motors are allowed on Kioshkokwi Lake.

RAIN LAKE

The Rain Lake access point is located 35 kilometres east of Emsdale on Highway 11. The entrance road is unpaved and the small campground has only basic facilities. The Park office sells permits and a few publications.

Rain Lake provides access not only to canoe routes but also to the Western Uplands Backpacking Trail. Motorboats with a maximum of 10-horsepower motors are allowed on the lake.

SHALL LAKE

Shall Lake lies 24 kilometres north of Madawaska on Highway 60. The access road is, for the most part, unpaved. There are no drive-in campgrounds or other facilities here except for the office, which sells permits and a few publications.

The highlight here, though, lies in the easy canoe routes that are accessed from Shall Lake. Some very scenic lakes, such as Shirley and Booth, can be reached with minimal portaging. Many historical sites, including a ranger cabin on Kitty Lake, are within easy access. A total of 10 "paddle-in" campsites (areas located a short distance from a drive-in location) are situated on Crotch

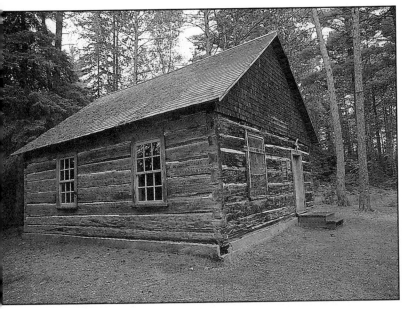

Only a handful of ranger cabins such as this one on Kitty Lake remain intact.

Lake only a few minutes' paddling time from the canoe launch. Motorboats are not allowed on these waters.

THE PARK INTERIOR

A canoe trip lasting for several days or longer gives one the opportunity to experience Algonquin at its best. To awaken in a dew-covered tent to the sleepy whistles of a White-throated Sparrow allows you to savour the new day as countless thousands of earlier explorers did. To watch a sinking sun set the waters ablaze while the rising wails of loons echo off distant hills is to discover the essence of the Park. Camping in the Park Interior bonds you with the wild in an intimate and unequalled way.

You need not be either an expert canoeist or experienced camper to explore the Park Interior. Common sense and a bit of preparation is all that is required. The outfitters are usually willing to advise you on which equipment will best suit your needs and which routes might be within your time budget. The Park interpretive and Canoe Centre staffs are well versed in Interior travel and are also worth seeking advice from.

Designated campsites are situated along most waterways throughout the Interior. Each has a fire pit as well as a privy of some sort. A maximum of nine people are permitted to camp at a single site. Since all access points limit the number of parties permitted entry each day, it is recommended to reserve access in advance. The Reservation Office number is provided in the appendix **IMPORTANT SERVICES**. The permit-issuing offices for each access point are listed in the *Canoe Routes of Algonquin Provincial Park* map brochure. Remember that in the Interior cans and bottles are banned.

The chapter **TIPS FOR THE EXPLORER** offers a few basic camping tips. The *Canoe Routes of Algonquin Provincial Park* map brochure is certainly a must for both navigating and camping in the Interior. Also, the map brochure is an important tool for enhancing a canoe trip, since it identifies areas of natural history and historical interest. Another extremely useful Park publication concerning Interior use is the free tabloid *Algonquin Provincial Park: The Park Interior.*

Wildlife-viewing Areas

Wildlife can certainly be encountered on any Interior trip. However, some areas are particularly good for certain species. The following is a brief summary of some of the better locations for seeing animals.

Hailstorm Creek

This extensive boggy creek lies at the northwest corner of Opeongo Lake. To get there can be tricky, for Opeongo is the largest lake in Algonquin and can be extremely rough at times. There is a water taxi service available at the outfitters on Opeongo Lake.

The shallow creek is a favoured moose-feeding area. I have seen as many as 24 moose at one time eating here. Early summer is certainly the best time to see these giants. The creek is also an excellent place to view otters.

Another feature of this boggy area and the next one is the presence of nesting birds that are typically found in farmland outside the Park. Bobolinks and Savannah Sparrows thrive in these large open areas.

Grassy Bay

This boggy creek extending west from the south end of Trout Lake is similar to Hailstorm Creek in habitat but is less productive for moose.

Tim River

This meandering river on the West Side of the Park is excellent for moose in early summer. It also harbours otters as well as many species of northern birds.

Nipissing River

Like the Tim River, this winding waterway is excellent for moose and otters. The stretch between Cedar and Nadine lakes is particularly good.

Catfish Lake

This lake is an important one for moose calving in mid-May and is also significant as a feeding area in early summer. The large boggy marsh between Catfish and Sunfish lakes is excellent for moose and other wildlife in summer.

McCarthy Creek

This creek lies at the southwest corner of Booth Lake. Virtually every species of aquatic plant known in Algonquin is found here. This rich array attracts moose in early summer.

Hogan Lake

The huge boggy marsh at the southwest end is an excellent summer moose-feeding site.

Other Areas of Natural Significance

A few of the more outstanding areas of natural significance are given here.

Crow River White Pines

This is one of only two areas that still have virgin white pines standing. These magnificent 35-metre-tall trees tower above the nearby hardwoods and can be found approximately two kilometres south of the Crow River just east of Crow Lake.

Dividing Lake White Pines

This is the other area where virgin white pines still grow. Dividing Lake is situated on the southwest border of Algonquin, south of Smoke and Ragged lakes.

Dickson Lake Red Pines

While not as tall as the virgin white pines at Crow and Dividing lakes, the red pines growing on the east side of Dickson Lake are the oldest trees in Algonquin. They are now over 340 years old.

Historical Points of Interest

Due to the vast number of logging camp ruins and other relics from the early days in the Park an entire volume would be needed to cover all of the historical points of interest. Many of these have either become next to impossible to find or can be reached only with extreme effort. The following is simply a listing of some of the more obvious structures that one can easily access during Interior trips.

Barnet Depot and Alligator at Burntroot Lake

Depots were the administrative and supply headquarters for logging companies. Frequently farms were established at these sites to grow potatoes for the men and oats and hay for the horses.

The depot on the southwest shore of Burntroot Lake was built in 1890 by the Barnet Lumber Company and was used until at least 1912. A root cellar and the remains of an alligator are still easily located.

Alligator at Catfish Lake

Parts of an alligator are visible on the island in the northeast corner of Catfish Lake.

Ranger Cabin at Kitty Lake

This cabin, still in excellent condition, was used as a stopover for Park rangers during patrols for poachers and fires.

Ranger Cabin at McKaskill Lake

This cabin is maintained and remains in good shape.

Dennison Farm — East Arm of Opeongo Lake

This farm was cleared in the 1870s by Captain John Dennison, who was killed in 1881 by a black bear caught in a trap and was buried at the farm. The Dennison family moved out of the Park in 1882. The Fraser Lumber Company took over the farm and ran it for a number of years as a depot farm.

Du Fond Farm — Manitou Lake

Ignace and Francis Du Fond cleared this site in 1888. For income they sold produce to logging operations. The farm, which was the last one to be privately owned in the Park, was abandoned in 1916.

McLachlin Depot — Trout Lake

The remains of this depot, built about 1900 by the McLachlin Lumber Company, lie at the northeast corner of Trout Lake.

BRENT
MAP 16

GILMOUR LAKE

TECUMSEH LAKE

BRENT CRATER TRAIL

BRANT LAKE

MUSKWA LAKE

GHOST LAKE

RANA LAKE

CEDAR LAKE

BRENT

MAJOR ROAD · · · · · · · HIKING TRAIL ▱ OUTFITTING
SECONDARY ROAD 〜〜〜 RIVER ⌂ STORE
· · · · LOGGING ROAD 〜〜 STREAM 〖 PHONE
┼┼┼ RAILWAY LINE · — · — · PARK BOUNDARY
△ CAMPGROUND $ PERMITS/INFORMATION

KIOSK
MAP 17

LAUDER LAKE

AMABLE DU FOND RIVER

CURLY LAKE

KIOSK

$ △ 〖

BOULTER LAKE

KIOSHKOKWI LAKE

RAIN LAKE
MAP 18

RAIN LAKE

MACKINAW LAKE

LITTLE McCRANEY LAKE

McCRANEY CREEK

McCRANEY LAKE

MAJOR ROAD
LOGGING ROAD
RAILWAY LINE
CAMPGROUND
RIVER
STREAM
PARK BOUNDARY
HYDRO LINE
PERMITS/INFORMATION

SHALL LAKE
MAP 19

CROTCH LAKE

KITTY LAKE

FARM LAKE

SHALL LAKE

BOOTH LAKE

BILLY LAKE

ORAM LAKE

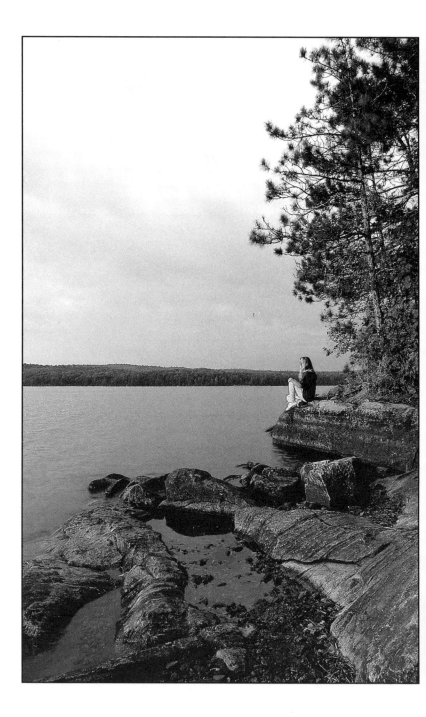

ALGONQUIN PROVINCIAL PARK is truly a mystical place. Whether it be the wails of a loon rising into the night, the splash of a bull moose munching watershield, the tracks of a wandering wolf crossing soft sand or the scarlet leaves of a red maple blazing against a September sky, the infinite facets of the Park never cease to captivate us. For those who explore its wild reaches Algonquin rewards with an endless array of life-long memories.

But the Park offers more than just natural wonders. Rotting timbers bordering bubbling creeks, mysterious openings in the forest, silent crosses marking unkempt graves — no matter where we roam remnants of another era can be discerned. Like clues in a mystery novel, these markers of a bygone era fuel our imagination and lead us into the past.

If this was your first excursion into Algonquin, I sincerely hope you had the good fortune to experience some of its magic. For anyone who proudly terms himself or herself a "regular," I know you have already fallen under Algonquin's spell. But whether you are making your first or 100th visit, if this book allowed you to leave the Park with an additional fond memory or two, or helped you to avoid a less than desirable experience during your stay, then it has fulfilled its purpose.

May you continue to enjoy this fabulous Park through all the years ahead.

Appendix 1 — Important Services

OUTFITTING SERVICES

For outfitters inside the Park the lake on which they are situated is given in brackets. For those outside the Park the nearest town is given. Complete outfitting is provided by all except those marked with an asterisk.

Oufitters within Algonquin

Algonquin Outfitters
(Cedar Lake)
RR #1, Highway 60
Dwight, Ontario
P0A 1H0
705-BRENT-0150
705-635-2243

Opeongo Algonquin
(Opeongo Lake)
RR #1, Highway 60
Dwight, Ontario
P0A 1H0
613-637-2075 (summer)
705-635-2243 (winter)

Alquon Ventures, Inc.
(Canoe Lake)
c/o Huntsville P.O.
Huntsville, Ontario
P0A 1K0
705-633-5622 (summer)
705-789-3645 (winter)

Outfitters outside Algonquin

Algonquin Outfitters (Dwight)
RR #1, Highway 60
Dwight, Ontario
P0A 1H0
705-635-2243

Algonquin Canoe Routes (Whitney)
Box 187
Whitney, Ontario
K0J 2M0
613-637-2699

Opeongo Outfitters (Whitney)
Box 123
Whitney, Ontario
K0J 2M0
613-637-5470

Algonquin Portage Store (Pembroke)
RR #6
Pembroke, Ontario
K8A 6W7
613-735-1795

Kanukawa Outfitters
(Deep River)
Box 115, RR #31,
Deep River, Ontario
K0J 1P0
613-584-2411

*Halfway Chute Canoe Rental
(Mattawa)
RR #2, Highway 630
Mattawa, Ontario
P0H 1V0
705-744-2155

157

Valley Ventures (Deep River)	Voyageur Outfitting

Valley Ventures (Deep River)
Box 1115
551 Highway 17 West
Deep River, Ontario
K0J 1P0
613-584-2577
or
RR #1, Braeside, Ontario
K0A 1G0
613-623-7166

Voyageur Outfitting
(South River)
Box 346, Station K
Toronto, Ontario
M4P 2G7
416-488-6175
or
Box 69
South River, Ontario
P0A 1X0

Canadian Wilderness Trips
(South River)
187 College Street
Toronto, Ontario
M5T 1P7
416-977-5763

Northern Wilderness Outfitters
(South River)
Box 89
South River, Ontario
P0A 1X0
705-386-0466
705-474-3272

*Poplar Point Camp (Kearney)
Box 99
Kearney, Ontario
K0A 1M0
705-636-5484

*Rickwards Small Motors (Kearney)
Box 224
Kearney, Ontario
K0A 1M0
705-636-5956

ACCOMMODATION

Only those lodges and motels found either inside or within 20 kilometres of Algonquin will be listed. Of course, numerous other places outside of this arbritrary distance offer accommodation. I would suggest that you contact the Ontario Ministry of Tourism if additional information is required.

Accommodation within Algonquin

Arowhon Pines Lodge	705-633-5661	or	416-483-4393
Bartlett Lodge	705-633-5543		
Killarney Lodge	705-633-5551	or	416-482-5254
	(summer)		(winter)

Accommodation outside Algonquin

Algonquin Area Bed and Breakfast
Whitney, Ontario K0J 2M0   613-637-5387

Algonquin East Gate Motel
Box 193
Whitney, Ontario K0J 2M0   613-637-2652

Algonquin Parkway Inn
Box 237
Whitney, Ontario K0J 2M0   613-637-2760

Bear Trail Inn Resort
Box 158
Whitney, Ontario K0J 2M0   613-637-2662

Hay Lake Lodge
Box 189
Whitney, Ontario K0J 2M0   613-637-2675

Riverview Cottages
Box 29
Whitney, Ontario K0J 2M0   613-637-2690

Whitney Cabins
Box 15
Whitney, Ontario K0J 2M0   613-637-2626

Algonquin Inn and Roadhouse
RR #1
Dwight, Ontario P0A 1H0   705-635-2434   800-387-2244

Blue Spruce Inn
RR #1
Dwight, Ontario P0A 1H0   705-635-2330

Clover Leaf Cottages
RR #1
Dwight, Ontario P0A 1H0   705-635-2049

Curv-Inn
RR #1
Dwight, Ontario P0A 1H0   705-635-1892

Dwight Village Motel/Coffee Shop
Box 15
Dwight, Ontario P0A 1H0   705-635-2400

Lakewoods 4 Season Resort
RR #1
Dwight, Ontario P0A 1H0   705-635-2087

Logging Chain Lodge
Box 170
Dwight, Ontario P0A 1H0   705-635-2575

Nor' Loch Lodge
Box 29
Dwight, Ontario P0A 1H0   705-635-2231   800-565-2231

Oxtongue Lake Cottages
RR #1
Dwight, Ontario P0A 1H0   705-635-2951

Parkway Cottage Resort
RR #1
Dwight, Ontario P0A 1H0   705-635-2763

Riverside Motel/Restaurant
Dwight, Ontario P0A 1H0   705-635-1677

Spring Lake Motel/Restaurant
RR #1
Dwight, Ontario P0A 1H0   705-635-1562

Timber Trail Algonquin
RR #1
Dwight, Ontario P0A 1H0   705-635-1097   800-463-2995

White Birches Cottage Resort
RR #1
Dwight, Ontario P0A 1H0   705-635-2322

IMPORTANT ADDRESSES AND PHONE NUMBERS

For information or reservations by mail write to the address given for
the park superintendant.

Park Superintendent
Algonquin Provincial Park
Ministry of Natural Resources
Box 219
Whitney, Ontario
K0J 2M0
613-637-2780

Camping Reservations
705-633-5538/5725

Park Information
705-633-5572

Algonquin Park Visitor Centre
613-637-2828

The Friends of Algonquin Park
P.O. Box 248
Whitney, Ontario
K0J 2M0
613-637-2828

Emergency Telephone Numbers

Ontario Provincial Police
800-267-8919

Ambulance
Zenith 90000

Huntsville Hospital
705-789-2311

Barry's Bay Hospital
613-756-3044

Park Staff (8:00 a.m. to 4:30 p.m.)
613-637-2780
705-633-5572

Ontario Poison Control
800-267-1373

Fire (8:00 a.m. to 6:00 p.m.)
613-637-5422

Appendix 2 — Important Publications

The following is a list of important publications that deal with Algonquin Park. Many other excellent publications are now out of print; only those currently available are given. Because The Friends of Algonquin Park have produced such an excellent series of inexpensive books dealing with Algonquin, a separate section is devoted to these. Other published books appear in the next section.

THE FRIENDS OF ALGONQUIN PARK PUBLICATIONS

I highly recommend these publications as excellent sources of information on specific aspects of Algonquin. Not only are they exceptionally well done but they are also incredibly inexpensive. For example, *Birds of Algonquin Provincial Park* contains 89 colour photographs and in 1993 sold for a mere $2.95 plus tax.

I also suggest that you purchase the entire set of trail guides. In addition to being essential aids for full enjoyment of the self-guiding trails, they also offer lots of good information about the Park's natural and human history.

Natural History

Birds of Algonquin Provincial Park (Strickland)

Checklist and Seasonal Status of the Birds of Algonquin Provincial Park (Tozer)

Mammals of Algonquin Provincial Park (Strickland)

Wolf Howling in Algonquin Provincial Park (Strickland)

Wildflowers of Algonquin Provincial Park (Strickland and Levay)

Checklist of the Vascular Plants of Algonquin Provincial Park (Brunton and Crins)

Trees of Algonquin Provincial Park (Strickland)

Mushrooms of Algonquin Provincial Park (Thorn)

Checklist of the Conspicuous Fungi of Algonquin Provincial Park (Thorn)

Checklist of the Lichens of Algonquin Provincial Park (Dickson and Crins)

Checklist of the Bryophytes of Algonquin Provincial Park (Crins and Darbyshire)

Reptiles and Amphibians of Algonquin Provincial Park (Strickland)

Checklist of the Butterflies of Algonquin Provincial Park (Reynolds)

Human History

Algonquin Logging Museum Guidebook (Strickland)

A Pictorial History to Algonquin Provincial Park (Tozer and Strickland)

A Chronology of Algonquin Provincial Park (MacKay)

Early Days in Algonquin Park (Addison)

Glimpses of Algonquin (Garland)

Miscellaneous

Voices of Algonquin (Tozer and Gibson)

Names of Algonquin (Garland)

Acid Rain in Algonquin Provincial Park (Strickland)

A Flock of Ravens (Strickland and Rutter)

Fishing in Algonquin Provincial Park (Strickland)

The Canoeist's Manual (Stringer and Gibson)

A White-water Guide to the Petawawa River (Drought)

Canoe Routes of Algonquin Provincial Park (Strickland)

Backpacking Trails of Algonquin Provincial Park (Strickland)

OTHER PUBLICATIONS

The following are publications produced by publishers other than The
Friends of Algonquin Park. The name of the publishing company
appears in brackets after the name of the author.

Natural History

Algonquin Seasons — Runtz (Stoddart)

Moose Country — Runtz (Stoddart)

Human History

A Few Rustic Huts — Gage (Mosaic Press)

Over the Hills to Georgian Bay — MacKay (Stoddart)

Algonquin — MacKay and Reynolds (Boston Mills)

Miscellaneous

Algonquin: The Park and Its People — Stanfield and Lundell
(McClelland and Stewart)

Path of the Paddle — Mason (Key Porter)

Song of the Paddle — Mason (Key Porter)

logging: history of, 3-4, 35-36, 75, 84, 112-113, 115-116, 120-121, 133, 137-140, 148-150
logging remains, 51, 71-72, 73, 74, 75, 85, 100, 118, 123, 125, 137
Lookout Trail, 38, 67, 90
Loon, Common, 64-65; Brewer Lake, 65; Costello Lake, 65; Lake of Two Rivers, 65; Smoke Lake, 65
Lower Spectacle Lake, 123, 130
Lower Twin Falls, 78

MacDonald, J. E. H., 83
MacDougall, Frank A., 72
Mackinaw Lake, 152
Madawaska River, canoe route, 79-80; Common Merganser, 79; otter, 53
Mallard Lake, 94, 127
Manitou Lake, 149
maps, 87-92, 127-132, 141, 151-152
McCarthy Creek: moose, 147
McDonald Creek, 123, 130; moose, 123
McDonald family, 137
McKaskill Lake: ranger cabin, 149
McLachlin Lumber Company, 121, 139, 140, 150
McManus Lake, 94, 125-126, 127, 128
McManus Lake Road: Black-backed Woodpecker, 109; Gray Jay, 108; wolf, 102
McRae Lumber Company, 73, 74, 139
McRaney Creek, 152
McRaney Lake, 152
memorials and cairns, 72, 73, 74, 83, 137, 138, 140
Merganser, Common, 64; Madawaska River, 79; Oxtongue River, 77
Merlin, 110; Achray, 110; Lake Travers, 110, 125
Mew Lake, 89; beaver, 52; campground, 37, 43, 44, 45, 59; Gray Jay, 59; otter, 53
Mike's Bog: Spruce Grouse, 57
mink: Costello Creek, 82
Minnesing Lodge, 41
Minnesing Road, 41
Minnesing Trail, 39, 41, 89
Mizzy Lake: otter, 53
Mizzy Lake Trail, 37, 46, 69, 88; Black-backed Woodpecker, 60; birds, 54; Gray Jay, 59; moose, 48; otter, 53; Spruce Grouse, 56;
Molly Island, 85
moose, 9, 11, 17, 47-48; Achray Trail System, 99; Basin Road, 134-135; Beaver Pond Trail, 48; Berm Lake Trail, 99; Bonnechere River, 135,

140; Catfish Lake, 147; Costello Creek, 82; Fork Lake, 86; Hailstorm Creek, 147; Highway 60, 48; Hogan Lake, 148; Lake Travers, 100, 124, 125; Madawaska River, 79; McCarthy Creek, 147; McDonald Creek, 123; Mizzy Lake Trail, 48; Nipissing River, 147; Norway Lake, 86; Pretty Lake, 100; Sunday Creek, 86; Tim River, 147
motorboats, 44, 80, 82, 83, 121, 143, 144
Mowat, 84
Mowat Lodge, 84
muskrat: Lake Travers, 124; Madawaska River, 79
Muskwa Lake, 151

Nadine Lake, 147
Nighthawk, Common, 111
Nipissing River: moose, 147; otter, 147
Nominigan Lodge, 85
Northern Lights, 8
Norway Lake, 86, 90

Ooze Lake, 124, 130
Opalescent Lake, 124
Opeongo Lake, 52, 53, 75, 77, 81, 82, 90, 146, 149
Opeongo Road, 75, 82; Black-backed Woodpecker, 60; bear, 51; beaver, 52; Gray Jay, 59; moose, 48; otter, 53; Spruce Grouse, 56-57; wolf, 49
Opeongo Store, 43, 52, 76, 80
Oram Lake, 152
Osprey: Stratton Lake, 123
Ottawa, Arnprior and Parry Sound Railway, 4, 39, 37, 68-71, 79, 84, 86
otter, 9, 16, 53, 105-106; Basin Road, 136; Bonnechere River, 140; Costello Creek, 53, 82; Costello Lake, 53; Forbes Creek, 105; Hailstorm Creek, 147; Lake Travers, 106, 124; Lake Travers Road, 105-106; Little Madawaska Picnic Ground, 53; Madawaska River, 53, 79; Mew Lake, 53; Mizzy Lake Trail, 53; Nipissing River, 147; Pretty Lake, 106; Ring-neck Pond, 53; Stratton Lake, 123
Out-Side-In cabin, 97, 114
Owl, Barred, 15, 45, 60, 61-63, 110-111; Achray Road, 111; Barron Canyon Trail, 111; Brewer Lake, 63; Hardwood Hill, 62; Hemlock Bluff Trail, 62; Lake Travers

166